Alchemizing

Judgment

A Guide Back to Love

Avelin Crew,
    What a blessing to be with
you in your space. I am
so happy & grateful to call
you friends & soul family.
    Thank you for your
Kindness & generousity.

Abigail Gazda

All my love
Abigail

abigailgazda.com

PINA PUBLISHING 🍍 SEATTLE

The stories and events that appear in this book are true.

Text copyright © 2020 by Abigail Gazda
Cover design by Emily Gazda © 2020 by Abigail Gazda
Cover photo by Rebecca Root © 2020 by Abigail Gazda
Interior book design by Susan Harring © 2020 by Pina Publishing

For information about special discounts for bulk purchases contact:
sales@pinapublishing.com

Manufactured in the United States of America
Library of Congress Cataloging-in-Publication Data Gazda, Abigail.

Summary:
Simply put, this is a book about how to win the game of life.
This comprehensive guidebook is dedicated to helping you to tap into the endless wellspring of abundance and finally lays out the how-to of manifestation with many perspectives, exercises, and tools for becoming your highest and best.
Not only thought-provoking and applicable, this personal development book teaches the imperative role of your existence, and guides you to harness all of your power to create your most inspired life.
This training manual for Alchemists exposes and discusses the unhealed aspects of your soul, that you may not know exist. This knowledge allows you the power to transcend barriers and obstacles that are blocking your blessings, guiding you into a life beyond standards and limiting constructs.

ISBN: 978-1-943493-36-4 (softcover)   978-1-943493-37-1 (ebook)

[Self-Help-Nonfiction, Transformation Nonfiction. Empowerment-Nonfiction. Ontological Coaching-Nonfiction. Memoir-Nonfiction]

Dedication

This book is dedicated to the ones in search.

It is to those in search of answers, guidance, hope, faith, evidence, help, love, clarity, support, and more.

I know you have diligently looked far and wide and you can rest now.

It is your time to stop seeking and start seeing that the truth you have been in search of exists within you.

This is your guidebook back to you.
Back to your heart.
Back to love.

I know your journey has taken you every which way, likely to many peaks and valleys.
You are a divine gift on this planet and the search is over.

You are perfect. You are whole. You are complete and your purpose on the planet is to live as the fully unleashed, most authentic version of who you already are at your core.

No more looking.
No more becoming.
No more fixing, changing, wishing, and hoping.

Just being.

Welcome home.
I am happy you are here.

Preface

Judgment cannot thrive where love grows.
Darkness cannot overshadow where light shines.
Nothing can stop the heart of an Alchemist.

Welcome to a book dedicated to guiding you to tap into the endless wellspring of love; primarily located in the center of your chest. This book took some personal initiations because once I received the inspiration to write it, I didn't exactly feel prepared to. "Who am I to consider myself such an authority on judgment, being unbiased, or lacking prejudice?" I feared this divine download and questioned God. "I am nowhere near perfect or immune to humanness and subjectivity."

Except, instead of dialoguing with God about it, I just put it low on my priority list and focused on other projects. My ego wanted to write a few other books before this one and I planned on writing this one in a few years' time, yet, it was just within a few months that I experienced mental, emotional, and spiritual growth spurts that would prepare me sufficiently to put these words to paper.

I have studied Buddhism, Taoism, Catholicism, Christianity, Vipassana, ontology, hypnotherapy, meditation, prayer, spirituality, and more. I will speak to you with my own version of spirituality; a combination of these studies, which I refer to as the 'Boomerang Brigade.' I believe that all titles we can come up with, such as God, Universe, Source Energy, Vortex, Consciousness, and any other can all be interchangeable, and I will certainly interchange them throughout this book. What I have come to understand is that all of us, no matter which Higher Power we select, refer to, and talk to, are ultimately speaking about infinite and unconditional love. Even in respect to the agnostic perspective, love is a cornerstone we can all relate to. Love is a practice we can all develop in our commitment to unity.

It is said by many spiritual teachers, mentors, and gurus that whichever you pick is just fine. Just choose what works for you in service of your connection with the source of love. Beware, it is the constant hopping and switching of practices that never allows you to go to the depths in which you hit this wellspring of truth. Never getting too serious about any one form of guidance can turn out to be a trick of the ego, with the intention that you never find truth. That habit will always keep you at the surface of relationships with others, yourself, this planet, and a Higher Power. This can trick you into feeling unsuccessful in your attempts to experience lasting and meaningful connection, so once you find light on your path, follow it fully. This is the journey to the depths of your own internal guidance system. This is an inward journey, not a test of external factors.

If you stay at the surface of any construct you will stay in the construct of it. Any and all means of spirituality in their purest forms are meant to take you to the depths of your own heart to reach your soul and put it on loudspeaker. This book will help you do that. This book will deconstruct any constructs that prevent you from getting back to love. I will do this by dissecting and explaining the various components of going inward to turn anything and everything back into love.

Day in and day out, it is your job and mission to get back to love, so that you may unleash it on this world. As you may see in your daily life, at a societal or global level, this world always needs more love. It is never in shortage, and yet, we are trapped in our scarcity mind-sets that prevent us from receiving it fully. This book will help you harness it for yourself, so that you may facilitate its expansion in the world.

I like to imagine the Universe as a giant, mirrored room. Now, combine that visual with the concept that what you put out is reflected back to you. I invite you to experience your whole world as a giant, mirrored room, reflecting your energy. If you pay closer attention, you will be able to see in yourself the things that are coming at you in life. You will be able to identify how you source your life experience and how to become the deliberate creator of this experience.

This entire book will be about you, your energy, actions, reactions, and responsibility to put more love in the world. It will be about the work it takes for you to be able to put more love into the world. As a result, you will find yourself effortlessly receiving it back. If you take this guide seriously, you will be surrounded by love in any and every circumstance. You will find love in any and every person. I will teach you how to receive any-thing and transmute it into love, and in turn, abundance.

The work, skill, finesse, and mastery of an Alchemist will be thoroughly explained throughout this book. What I would like to share in this preface is that you have the power and ability to alchemize. By definition, this means to turn one thing into another. By definition of this book, it is to turn everything into love.

When I first received the message to write this book, the human Abigail felt fear and insecurity. I began to think of times I have, and still judge harshly. I began to recall hurtful thoughts, words, and actions that have revealed my prejudices. I definitely did not feel like I was the perfect person to channel and deliver this information.

Maybe a saint, preacher, or world leader? I had resistance to being the one to bring this brilliance to you. Can you guess why? For fear of judgment!

I was afraid that if I positioned myself as an authority on this topic, I would be singled out for the times my judgment has impacted others. I was nervous that people would ridicule, criticize, or question the methodology I am about to present to you. I was definitely unsure about my future and how I might be pinned to an identity that is expected to be judgment-free, completely tolerant, all loving, and utterly accepting. This felt daunting when this book started pushing its way through my being.

Here is what I now know as a result of God's work in me. The contents of this book have been channeled through me as a vessel of divine intelligence. While I enjoy putting my name on the front of these books, the messages I have published could have come through any one of us. It is time the world receives this concept explained this way. I happen to be the one allowing it to come through at his moment in humanity's timeline.

As for this Abigail body, I am human. By way of being human, I am subjective. I have a thinking brain that calculates and makes predictions and assumptions. It is impossible for humans not to judge, perceive, react, and more. I am certain that as a human, I will make many mistakes and react impulsively for the rest of my life.

The work of an Alchemist is more a career or craft than a study-for-the-test type of knowledge. It is wisdom to be attained and applied moment by moment. You will have thousands of opportunities every single day to hone and utilize alchemy.

I now understand that I was guided to write Alchemizing Judgment for exactly that reason. We will never be without judgment. To eliminate it is impossible and futile to plan for. Our task and challenge is to take full responsibility for our judgments and transmute them into energy that empowers all living beings.

Acknowledging and accepting what is, without the immediate impulse to fix or change it, is a sign of emotional maturity that will afford you the opportunity to morph barriers into stepping stones of progress. In this book, I will share with you many perspectives, exercises, and tools for being a contribution to the evolution of humanity.

Some of you may not feel called into global leadership or care much about policy and reform. That is perfectly fine. What is important to remember is that doing your job to the best of your ability is your contribution to the evolution of humanity.

This may look like raising healthy, empowered, conscious children. This may be owning a local, small business that serves the community you live in. This could look like being present in your profession and making hearts lighter around you. It might be as simple as picking up trash when you see it and holding a door open for someone else. It can be visiting the elderly and reminding your loved ones how important they are to you.

I will explain in this book the utter importance of your existence and how nothing here is a mistake. The Universe is intricate and interlocking, and there is no job too big or too small. We can teach our children how important they are in this evolution, too. We can begin to respect our fellow beings, our brothers and sisters on this planet, as an extension of ourselves. Remember that mirrored room? Yeah. We are intertwined in our purpose, and to use alchemy to our fullest capacity shall bring us all further down the path of fulfillment, peace, and enlightenment.

As you read this book, it is my prayer for you that you come to understand your own divinity and purpose on this planet. I pray you find clarity in these pages, that opens your heart and mind to what is possible when we truly see our oneness. I hope you find powerful guidance and utilize it to practice your shifts out of fear and into love. Yes, shifts. There are many. I pray you grant yourself complete grace as you try and try again.

This is a process, my love.

Transformation is not about being fixed forever. It is about staying empowered more frequently and for longer durations. You will feel disempowered at points. You will trip and fall. You will judge again. You will have a negative impact again. This book will teach you what to do when you do, and how to clean up any messes made in the process.

By the end of this book, you will understand the three most important pillars of life: integrity, alignment, and faith. You will feel empowered to live with your heart unleashed. You will understand yourself in a whole new way that feels exciting. You will see new perspectives of possibility for yourself, humanity, and this world. You will feel clearer, lighter, ready, and willing to alchemize judgment and be a part of the walk back to love.

I want to thank you for picking up this book. I have no doubt it is in divine order and I have complete trust that it is perfect for you at this time. May these pages unleash that beautiful heart of yours.

Namaste.

Table of Contents

Chapter 1

Understanding Alchemy

Before diving face first into a concept that may be a bit unclear, I would like to set the stage for the conversation that this book will inspire.

We weren't exactly taught alchemy in school. Unless you had a special focus on science or philosophy, the concept of alchemy may be somewhat foreign to you. I'd like to take a moment to build a context for this transformation we are looking to create.

As explained briefly in the preface, alchemy is to change one thing into another. From a scientific standpoint, that often looks like changing metals into other metals. This process is often used to turn base metals into precious metals. This can be an exciting idea, with the prospect of turning less sought after metals into gold. It is a constructive use of resources to create a desired outcome.

I like the idea of sharing the scientific definition, because from the philosophical standpoint, we are turning less desirable thoughts, feelings, and emotions into gold as well; the high vibrational and ever-valuable material of love!

Although we are discussing philosophical and existential alchemy, it isn't meant to remain some intangible concept, especially for the purposes of this book. In order to truly experience the magic and mysticism of a concept, you actually have to take the magic and mysticism out of it first, and allow the concept to manifest itself. When we leave something a mystical mystery, we have no practical way of accessing or utilizing it with intention. Rather, we just hold our breath, click our heels, and hope that by chance it finds us. This won't get us where we want to go. Breaking down a process to fully understand it empowers you to apply it on purpose and experience the flow of being in that process.

According to the Greek etymology of the word alchemy, it is defined as "the process of transmutation by which to fuse or reunite with the divine or original form."

In this book, I will spend many pages explaining how the original form of every single thing is Love. Everything comes from one collective consciousness; one nucleus of energy. Anything that has manifested in this world is an extension and an authentic expression of that energy. Love energy comes through in countless forms, which I will explain thoroughly in this book. For now, I want to touch on the expression of energy, and how this causes manifestation.

Everything that has come into form is the expression

of someone's unique perspective, manifested through the process of creation. Even in nature, the way a tree grows or a canyon forms is an exclusive expression of the intricacies of its divine location, weather, and timing. From people to places, not one are alike, and yet, are all transmuting energy into matter.

Another word and concept that will arise often in this book is 'transmutation,' which means "to change or alter in form, appearance, or nature; especially to a higher form."

My favorite example of this is sexual transmutation. Sexual energy is a lower order expression of its origin, which is creative energy. Within the body, the epicenter of sexual and creative energy is the pelvis; the sacral chakra. We often default to using sexual activity to express and expend our creative energy when that is not its only use. It takes a mature understanding of these energies to also comprehend the higher order application of them. This also takes a notable amount of self-control. I am speaking rather collectively here, but at least in the Western world, the way that we have glorified sex and oversexualized the human bodies, creative expression naturally takes a back seat. Sex is one example that is also correlated to the focus on looks, attraction, and external validation, all of which take away from our focus on organic, creative endeavors.

Without more intentional training, young people are left to their own experiments and discoveries when it comes to this. I found this all too true as a Health and Wellness educator at the middle and high school level.

As an educator, I witnessed the difference between teaching 'Sex Ed' as a textbook unit as opposed to a life lesson. Young men and women knew very little about the consequences of sexual activity and even less about how to harness creative energy. They simply followed urges and attraction without considering the long term consequences of those actions.

I saw this countless times with students I taught. I saw it as a Resident Assistant in college, and still, today, as a coach. So many humans have simply not been taught that our sexual energy can be held and raised to an even higher frequency and used in a different manner to create something other than physical intimacy. Even in a relationship, physical connection isn't the highest form of connection. This is where we can elevate the quality of our relationships, as well. This kind of training also helps us to shift our focus off of another human and back onto ourselves for our self-love, worth, and inspiration. This naturally transforms our thought patterns from obsessing over relationships to a more balanced focus on other areas of life. Our creative energy is the vehicle that the love frequency uses to take form in our physical world. Therefore, if we only use the urge of creative energy on sex, we are spending our energetic currency in a way that can cost us more than it makes us.

Sex is great and I love great sex as much as anyone else. Sex is healthy in many ways, but we also have too many brilliant people who have not been taught to harness the creative energy that activates their reproductive organs. They have not been taught that what they feel in their pelvic region could actually be a book, painting, song, poem, invention, or more. We become pregnant with ideas and that level of inspiration is literally arousing. It is the arousing part that detours the untrained mind. An amateur creative can misunderstand this arousal for sexual desire, when they could have created something entirely different.

Children are the form that sexual energy manifests in our physical world. It is one means of creation. To intentionally harness our creative energy without expending it on sex can fuel us to produce other results we may have been struggling to previously manifest. Having a child can be someone's greatest blessing in life, especially when reproduction is the intention of sex. Children can also be a result of an impulsive decision based on creative urges mistaken as sexual desire.

When individuals are taught this and begin their own practice of deciphering sexual and creative energy, the possibilities become endless. I am an advocate for healthy sex, for sure. I am also an advocate for practiced abstinence as a means of more effectively utilizing creative energy. This isn't specifically taught in schools due to the taboo nature of having a conversation about sex. In most school settings, the bare minimum is covered as to move past the conversation and call it done as opposed to making sure our young people are given a true, in depth opportunity to understand puberty, maturation, sex, intimacy, reproduction, and more. When discussed with both young and old, I see their eyes widen with realization.

In the same way it is effective not to have a large wardrobe as to save your decision-making energy for more important choices throughout your day, saving your sexual energy for creative endeavors will empower you to produce results beyond your wildest dreams. You will be astonished by all your newfound clarity, energy, and inspiration. I can personally tell you that times when I practice abstinence or more intentional sexual activity, I can actually feel all of my power reeling back into my body. I can sense this restoration and use that energy on writing, speaking, coaching, and more.

Conversely, if I am expending sexual or creative energy recklessly, I struggle with feeling too exhausted for my passions. My projects suffer because I am feeling too drained to complete every task fully. It is predictable that when I am writing a book, my podcast takes a back seat. When I am launching a course, I am not writing a book. When organizing a retreat, I am not focused enough to acquire clients. When starting a new relationship, I must make sure not to surrender all of these projects for the excitement of kisses...because I am definitely prone to doing that. I am sharing this to explain that if you are not highly intentional with the expenditure of your energy, you *will* deplete yourself. Respecting this natural occurrence is a practice of self-mastery for the trained creative to be effective in delivering his or her gifts to the world without feeling exhausted by his or her own passions.

I am going into such detail on this topic because it is valuable to your creation, inspiration, and leadership.

This book will go into much further detail about you delivering your gifts to the world, and maintaining your power is imperative to the task. It is also imperative that all of this is fun and enlivening. It is about becoming the whole of who you came here to be. I am teaching you how to thrive, not survive. This book is about winning the whole game of life, not just one part of it. Sex, intimacy, and relationships are one part of life. You have a bigger game to play. You have a major gift to deliver. Becoming a master of your sexual and creative energies is a key to life I value greatly, because it wasn't until I understood this skill did I become fulfilled by both of them.

My favorite example may be sexual transmutation, but this works the same way with so many examples. Our actions are the vehicle that energy rides into this physical plane. To say it in the language of the Law of Attraction; what you focus on increases. I invite you to take inventory of how and where you are spending all of your energy.

Energy spent gossiping creates drama.

Energy spent drinking creates health, financial, career, and relationship issues.

Energy spent worrying creates physical and mental illness. Energy spent learning creates growth and opportunities.

Energy spent mastering a craft creates a master.

Energy spent expressing inspiration creates books, movies, music, art, and more.

The list goes on, and on.

Energy is everything. Everything you are doing is

a vehicle for energy to manifest into form. You may not even realize how powerful your every action is. It is not a question of *if* you are a creator, it is a matter of *how* you are a creator. When you become more serious about how and where you spend your energy, you will get to experience yourself as the creator of your life.

I have one more example of how much of a creator you are, and it's a fun one: Imagine your hands as garden hoses with no off valve. Always on, pouring water everywhere. If this were the case, sleeping in bed, being inside, or being in a car would be a mess! You would want to stay outside at all times. While you're out there, you might as well water the plants and the grass. You can even rinse the car and the patio. You can fill jugs and reservoirs. Once you get over any frustration you feel for having garden hoses as hands, you will find ways to give them purpose.

You have energy pouring out of your hands at all times. You could spill it all over the house, at the bar, at the movies, or at your friend's house. You could smear it on people, places, and things, or you could pour it onto a canvas. You could put it in pots and pans to make a delicious meal. You could attach a pen to that hand and harness and direct that energy to write your business plan or floor plan. You can find ways to use this ever-flowing energy *on* purpose and *with* purpose.

You are an Alchemist.

You have been all along.

It's time you step fully into your role.

It's time to become a deliberate creator.

Chapter 2

The Path Ahead

In my adult life, I have been an educator, coach, sponsor, manager, consultant, and more. I have been guiding humans for many years now. I have worked with hundreds of people in many stages of life. People have come to me with a wide variety of issues, ailments, or concerns, and an equally wide variety of dreams, visions, and goals. After working with so many people, the one thing that has become very clear to me is the process of transformation we all go through. While this varies in many ways, there are so many fundamental breakdowns and breakthroughs that we naturally evolve through that lead us to journey inward.

In my life coaching career, I am an emotional intelligence expert who focuses primarily on subconscious reprogramming. This practice ranges from inner child work, shadow work, integration, completion, forgiveness, surrender, leadership, and more. I refer to myself as a Clarity Coach because I help people obtain clarity about who they are, what they want, how to get there, how to identify what's in the way, and how to overcome what is in the way.

The process of transformation has become so predictable that I have developed an ability to identify exactly where a person is on their journey, and what lies ahead for them. I used to judge myself as pretentious for acting like I understood this information, until I realized it wasn't an act. I knew that I recognized this as wisdom, not as a regurgitation of information. I began to feel pretty mystical for knowing exactly when someone's ego was going to strike to sabotage all of their efforts and success. I knew when my clients were on the verge of a breakthrough based on all the breakdowns they were experiencing. I knew to teach them specific distinctions when I could sense they would be experiencing particular stages of growth.

I began to connect more to my own spiritual journey, because the exposure of performing this kind of work with others offered me the opportunity for perspective from a variety of individuals. I often felt like I was watching my life from an elevated place. Again, I'd judge myself for feeling that way. "You're not that special," I would hear my inner critic scathe. "Get over yourself," I would hear the inner voices of elders scorn. My clients' feedback and results would tell a different story, though. Witnessing the Phoenix Effect take place in each of their lives as they rose from the ashes of the tired, unfulfilled identities they showed up as brings tears to my eyes every single time. My own

Phoenix experience has occurred time and time again as I have continuously shown up for my purpose to lead and guide.

In my own growth and evolution, I have most deeply connected with the identity of Guardian Angel... and you guessed it, I have judged the heck out of myself for even daring to consider myself so important. On a soul level, I could sense my 'GA' self and would go inward to her when I was seeking the most unadulterated guidance. I have learned to embody her so much that my life has completely transformed in ways that have led me to write this book. I was not ready to write this book before accepting the identity of Guardian Angel. I was too scared. I was still confused. I was not in communion with God nor directly connected to Source Energy. I couldn't fully tap into Infinite Intelligence because I wouldn't let myself feel worthy enough. This didn't prove anything in the way of humility or grace. It was just me cutting myself and everyone around me off from all that is available in the full acceptance of our brilliance and radiance. I was not in the full embodiment of my own divinity that would therefore empower me to reflect yours.

If I had not learned to alchemize all of the judgment over the years of leaving academia, corporate environments, and high paying jobs to pursue entrepreneurship, I would not be where I am today. Through this growth, I have published multiple books, created a globally-downloaded podcast, cultivated a thriving coaching practice, developed health and wealth, and have reached the best relationship with myself and my life that I've ever had. If I didn't prioritize transmuting judgment into empowerment, I would still be feeling stuck, confused, hopeless, resigned, and resentful.

Throughout this book, I will teach you how to transmute the judgment of others. Most importantly, I will teach you how to identify and transmute the judgment occurring within, because this is the most lethal weapon you possess. It cuts you off from your connection to the Source. It constricts the flow of abundance and inspiration. It keeps you trapped in disempowerment and the illusions of this physical reality. It kills all hope and possibility of ever becoming anything you dream of.

Over the course of mastering my craft, I have identified some major stages of life and transformation that I would like to give you a brief understanding of. I will reference them in this book frequently, so that seeing the timeline for this process will make it more fun, free, effortless, and enjoyable. To see the path of enlightenment laid out affords you the opportunity to choose it intentionally at any given moment.

Some spiritual teachers believe the best teacher is silence, and in many cases, I agree. On the contrary, my journey has been accelerated by those willing to walk with me on my path and shine light where I could not see. Some simple explanations of complex obstacles have made the biggest differences in my life. I can recall clearing things up that had been bewildering me for years in just hour-long phone calls with a life coach. The inner work bends the laws of time and concrete reality. This makes exponential growth possible and very available. That is why I feel that explaining transformation clearly can encourage more people to take that first, magical step.

I find myself wishing that it didn't always have to take a traumatic awakening to shift people's consciousness. However, I see time and time again that many do not choose transformation until it is more uncomfortable to stay the same than it is to make a serious change. In this chapter, I will explain the steps that lead up to one choosing transformation, and the road ahead once you finally announce to yourself and the Universe, "I am ready."

There are three major stages of life that I see occur that lead up to someone's desire for transformation. Side bar: this is a fast forward to a person's young adult years. For the purposes of this lesson, I am skipping the formative years, when our brains are still developing and have yet to become our adult personalities. For more about this impressionable stage, get my book *Giving Up Giving Up: The Memoir of a Quitter.*

Beginning with the young adult years, first, there is the Shock and Awe phase, which I believe happens after we leave school and enter the workforce. This also tends to happen with the onset of a marriage, after having a first child, or the purchase of a first home. It is different for different people. However, the overall experience is, "Wait a minute! Nobody told me about this! What is this? Is *this* what this is like?!?" It's a general experience of bewilderment that the situation is nothing like we planned for it to be. We are shocked at what being an adult actually comprises of, and how totally unprepared we feel for it. This phase also includes feelings of betrayal, frustration, annoyance, disappointment, anxiety, resentment, despair, hopelessness, and more.

How long someone stays in the Shock and Awe phase has a lot to do with upbringing and emotional intelligence. For reference, emotional intelligence can also sometimes be considered 'common sense.' If young folks are shown that what they know as common sense is put down or criticized enough, they doubt themselves and begin to give up their own inner authority early, never learning how to harness it. We do not do our children any favors by teaching them that external authority is more important than their own internal guidance system.

Think about it. Someone did this to you, and you gave up your own inner authority, as well. It took years to finally take your power back and begin to trust your own intuition again…or maybe you are arriving to that conclusion at this very moment. Either way, it is never too late to make this shift.

The second phase is what I call Social Media Syndrome. I would likely have called this something different if I were from a different generation. However, in this day and age it is about trying to keep up with what we see in people's highlight reels and Instagram influencer's accounts. We spend years striving for an outdated American Dream type of illusion; the perfect house, relationship, career, car, family, etc. It's your version of what you consider as the 'white picket fence vision.' It's an illusion of perfection with a facade of achievement, when really, there is no fulfillment, joy, satisfaction, or peace available in this phase.

This is the phase that usually has us peak into our awakening. We get to those 'made it' and 'mountain top moments' only to discover other mountains off in the distance. In a defeated and exhausted fashion, we begin our descent, and head for the next one. We max out on trying to show off, people please, or prove ourselves that we end up causing breakdowns in our life as a result of lack of boundaries and sense of self.

We are trying to live up to someone else's standards of success. We chase these fantastic dreams until we have them, only to realize once we are there that it is a delusion. We find ourselves confused, disappointed, unsatisfied, lonely, afraid, anxious, and depressed. This is also the phase of deep depression and self-harm because life feels so confusing. "How can I have all that I've ever dreamed of wanting, and not want any of it?" This is a time of questioning all we have ever lived for and feeling as though we have wasted years, maybe even decades. We avoid considering starting over because that idea simply spirals us into fear, regret, and sadness. This phase can lead to substance abuse, sexual misconduct, debt, eroding relationships, numbing out, careless health choices, failure to perform at work, parenting issues, and whatever other ways we can deteriorate our lives.

This is what I meant when I said I wish I could

spare people the traumatic awakening experience. We have been so conditioned that hard work is the answer to achieving our happiness that we may climb dozens of those mountains before slowing down enough to say, "I am not happy," and surrendering the battle. We relentlessly force ourselves into such oblivion that we have no idea who we are anymore, or what we are working for. The shove out of this phase usually takes a divorce, job loss, near death experience, or death of a loved one that awakens us into the next stage of life, which I call the Enough is Enough phase.

I lovingly refer to the folks in this group as 'my people!' The Enough is Enough crowd has had it! They have had it with pretending. They are tired of trying to be anyone else. They are ready to be exactly who they are. They are done trying to please, impress, and run themselves ragged in the rat race.

The Enough is Enough phase is magical, because it is the phase in which someone is ready for transformation. They are willing to be worked with by a coach, a mentor, or a spiritual guide. In Shock and Awe and Social Media Syndrome, the person may be complaining a lot or tired but they're not ready to be told that it is their responsibility to make a shift. They are still stuck in blaming, shaming, and degrading. Judgment can really have a hold on people in these phases because they are still trying to compare and move up in the hierarchy.

When Enough is Enough hits, there is no more of that. It is enough of everything. Doing anything you don't want to do becomes intolerable and downright repulsive. This is predictably a stage of rebellion. Enough BS. Enough pretending. Enough living up to anything. This person accepts that if they're going to live a good life it is up to them, and they are fully ready to take responsibility for it. This is where disruption of the identity starts.

When people reach this stage, it is very explosive. They tend to want to demolish everything that is not working in their lives. They leave jobs, marriages, living environments, and more. They start telling people off and not really caring about others' opinions. This is healthy and natural, but it is not sustainable. The Enough is Enough phase is simply a milestone in transformation. It comes after the awakening and right before the meaningful introspection, which is what leads to true and lasting change.

Next, I will explain the work that I do with people. No matter when I meet them, they usually come to work with me in the Enough is Enough mentality and I take them through transformation into their true, authentic, and divine leadership. This work is a simple matter of evolution. Although these lessons may be taught, they must be applied to life in order to be fully integrated and personally internalized by the individual.

This process is not founded on instant gratification and cannot be completed in a few days or weeks. No matter how long it takes, or how slowly it goes, it is the most beautiful human experience to witness. I am honored to do the work I do with people who are ready to live the life they've been given.

The four stages of transformation that I guide individuals through are Self Discovery, Self Development, Self Mastery, and Transcendence.

Self Discovery is exactly what it sounds like. In this stage, a person has decided they're ready to be themselves. When faced with that decision, they have no idea who they are, what they want, or how to even get where they think they're going. This can be scary at first, especially when they realize they have been spending their whole lives living up to other people's expectations and standards.

This is an awakening time in itself because a person starts to see how far off they have strayed from their own value system. They really have no idea what their own definition of success is because they've been seeking the validation of others. They have been too busy trying to be some type of acceptable that they have morphed far away from their most original self. In this stage, there is a lot of unbecoming in order to truly become. Self Discovery is a beautiful phase where a lot of blossoming occurs.

The stage of Self Development is a very interesting one. I like to let anybody willing to listen know that the self development industry makes a lot of money off of you being unsure of yourself. It cashes in on your insecurities and uncertainties. I like to tell my clients that even if it is a few months or a few years, my job is to put myself out of business with you. I do not want to keep you coming back for more, trying to fix yourself because you think you're broken. You are not broken.

You simply have judgments about yourself, which are regurgitated thoughts you've heard your entire life, about how much the ideal person should weigh, what the societal norm of beauty is, or what kind of job to have, and how much salary you should be making each year. All of these are subtle judgments that we cast upon ourselves to measure our competency, our capability, and our capacity. These are not effective measures of who you are or your impact on the world.

This is why I like to walk people through the Self Development phase more quickly than the industry would 'recommend.' I have noticed that people get stuck on the self development wheel for decades and never come out knowing anything more about themselves, the human psyche, or this world. They just become addicted to the intellectual stimulation of self development and call it transformation.

When I identified this leg of transformation as a single phase and noticed the way that people get stuck in it, I decided to create a phase and course in Self Mastery. Self Mastery is an incredibly important stage that affords people the opportunity to understand that they are the master of themselves. This is the time for people to fully accept their humanness and begin to apply it as their means of relating to other humans, as a way to heal and guide. This becomes a true self-study phase, where the conscious you integrates the subconscious you as a tool. This gives a person a sustainable way to live their fullest life at their highest and best. When self mastery is employed, a person becomes unleashed to fulfill their purpose on the planet, because when you can master yourself, you can master humanity.

I believe that this phase is close to Buddhist practices of compassion, love, understanding, and acceptance. I work rigorously with clients to accept, love, celebrate, and unleash themselves. This is an important shift; millions of people spend the majority of their lives trying to find and fix what's wrong with them. If you insist that you are broken, you will always find evidence for that belief, because that is the filter you are looking through. My friend, you will always find what you are looking for. People search so long and hard for what's wrong with them that they never find out what's right with them. They never discover, harness, or deliver their gifts to this world because when they see glimpses of their greatness, they smother it with doubt, insisting that there is more work to be done before they can be great.

Don't get trapped in self development. The self development industry makes the most of its money on you spinning your wheels here. Not only is it sad to see, it's criminal. To keep people stuck in Self Development is a disservice to humanity. I have taken it very seriously to move people into Self Mastery, so that they may discover their authentic leadership and begin to master their craft of whatever they came to this planet to do.

Upon arriving at a mastery level of self and purpose on this planet, I like to take people through the last phase of transformation, which I call Transcendence. This is where the heart and soul take precedence over anything the human mind and body can prioritize. Transcendence is an elevation above our humanness that allows us to channel our divine guidance and apply it to this world.

This is a special phase, because while new age spirituality may be sexy, what I guide at this level is about your direct connection with your Higher Power. Many religions teach you *about* your God, but do you *actually* know him? Can you have your own conversations with God? Can you have your own connection with The Source from which you came? Can you hear him speaking directly to you, nourishing you, giving you inspired thoughts, giving you specific instructions, asking you to manifest evidence of love all over this world? Your willingness to channel Infinite Intelligence facilitates the awakening and evolution of humanity.

Transcendence is about levitating above our humanness in order to be the clearest vessel for Intelligence to flow through. When I suggest words and phrases such as transcending humanness, levitating, elevating, rising above, and other related concepts, I am not suggesting you place yourself on a pedestal above others that actually encourages separateness. I am not promoting a hierarchy for which to judge and assess someone's level of enlightenment. The humanness I am referring to transcending is our fallen human nature; the underdeveloped versions of us that lust, envy, compete, complain, and coerce. I am talking about cleaning up your act as a human in a way that allows you to level up in life towards a more whole, complete, and compassionate version of you that more seriously considers your contribution to humanity.

So much of this book is about your divine role here. Fulfilling your role effectively will require your transcendence above addictions of the body and mind, both physical and emotional. Our cravings and aversions to the positive and negative aspects of life are all distractions from true peace and harmony. Yes, positives. We become so addicted to positive reinforcement and material evidence of our worth that even many of the positive aspects of life feed on our primal human nature. I will teach you how to transcend these worldly treasures to experience the treasure that you are.

Another important facet of Transcendence is that it is not meant to put you above others. Often, when we elevate, we naturally experience a differentiation from our old ways of being. We separate ourselves from the way we used to be, believing that it was 'bad' or 'wrong.' This is just a phase. The more we heal, the more compassion we have for old, maybe unhealthy or destructive behaviors. The whole point of Transcendence is not to become some type of 'better than.' Rather, it is to rise up, gain perspective, and then get your feet back on the ground to be here on Earth as a walking, talking, living, breathing example of infinite love. It is a holy experience to be here as a shining presence of divinity and grace. You aren't meant to transcend to leave this planet. You are meant to rise up above barriers that prevent you from living out your wholeness and inspiring others to begin their journey. You are meant to transcend the way a beacon is meant to shine light, direct, and guide. Transcendence is an action of love in alignment with a commitment to Collective restoration.

I will teach you how to transcend lower frequency human habits that prevent you from reaching your fullest potential. Through this process, you will get to experience authentic and lasting joy. These are big promises, I know, but in my work, I have witnessed it occur time and time again. I have watched people come back to life and recognize the unadulterated power they have within.

At this level of your leadership, you become willing to give up all of your own worldly identities in order to identify with the oneness that we are. This doesn't mean you lose yourself. It means that you become restored to who and what you were made to be and to fulfill the divine role you came here to play. You will be in a direct connection with the truest, most authentic version of you. You will be in consistent alignment with your intuition and inner guidance system to navigate life here on Earth. This is that direct connection that Transcendence makes available. This book is about living in the stage of Transcendence.

You wouldn't be reading this if you weren't meant for more. We wouldn't have found each other here if your soul hadn't nudged you to this book. You have a direct connection to your source energy, and when you connect intentionally, you will be the most *in your purpose* and *on purpose* you have been in all of your life. Working with you in the stage of Transcendence to clarify who you are and what you are here to do, is the most phenomenal gift I can imagine getting to do with my own life. This is your calling, too. It is each of ours in our own right. How it manifests for you is yet to be discovered. This book will help you reach that clarity.

I have crafted these four major phases into a curriculum for transformation to prevent people from spending unnecessary time reaching around 'the dark room' of evolution. As mentioned earlier, working with a leader, mentor, or guide would 'flip on the light switch' for me and I would be empowered to navigate the next stage, highly aware of my surroundings. I credit my rapid growth and maturation to this work, and I take a lot of pride in offering it to those interested.

The topics in this book are relevant and important at every stage, and they take time. To alchemize judgment is not easy for the reactive mind. For the person who does not know themselves, judgment can cause doubt. To the person who has not accepted themselves, judgment can trigger insecurities and open wounds. You must be willing to transcend above your circumstances in such a way that they do not take you out on impact. All of these factors can cloud your judgment and prevent you from recognizing the opportunity at hand; to generate more love in the world.

Being able to alchemize judgment the moment it is presented will grant you the superpower of finding value in every moment of every day. Judgment is always a gift to meet ourselves and others more fully. You will be invited to meet yourself in ways you have never considered before. This will require your willingness to remain receptive to new perspectives and challenges. In this book, I will invite you to be the most open-hearted you have ever been and remind you that it is safe to do so.

No judgment can harm you, my friend. It is one of your greatest teachers, and teachers serve the purpose of providing knowledge and education. It is your duty to learn the art of transmuting all energies into love so that you may always be offering the highest and best you have to offer; unconditional grace, love, and gratitude.

I am so excited to take this journey with you. Let's begin.

Chapter 3

Winning the Game of Life

The core of this book will be broken down into three major sections that will teach you how to win the game of life. As you may have been able to discern by now, I am not interested in simply *surviving* life. I am invested in each and every human being absolutely *thriving* in life. What I can deduce from you making it to this page is that you have the same vested interest in this whole 'livin' ya best life' gig. I am glad we can agree on that, and I am so excited to offer you information that will put you in the fast lane to reaching it.

When it comes to thriving, I have identified these three elements of life to be of the utmost importance, and I will share with you why prioritizing them will set you up for success. If you are aware of these aspects, the negative effect can be subtle and slippery. You may just feel 'in a funk' or struggling through a slump you can't seem to get out of. Maybe you have never been able to catch your stride or cross the threshold into true and lasting success. Taking responsibility for these three areas of your life will transform all of that. I will share these aspects as pillars of your highest and best life, and they consist of Integrity, Alignment, and Faith.

Becoming one hundred percent responsible for your awareness around these three pillars will have your life going smoothly, so that instead of being consumed by your past, judgments, fears, or struggles, you will be free to live a life that leaves a true legacy. I believe that if we were operating with full freedom, power, and self-expression, we would be far more interested in delivering our service to the world as our contribution to the evolution of humanity.

Often when I talk about our contribution to humanity, people get a bit skittish about how much they might be expected to contribute. I hear, "I just want a happy family," or "I am not trying to start some company that changes the world." I get that. That is not what each person is called to do. Keep in mind that living at your healed, highest, and best *is* your contribution to humanity.

To whatever scale we each desire, we can contribute to the Collective evolution. We exist to express ourselves creatively and be productive in ways that bring us joy and fulfillment. If everyone on the planet were operating in this fashion, everyone would be fulfilling their unique role and satisfying their own needs and each other's. I will go into much more depth about this concept as we dive deeper into this book. As for this chapter, I want to give you a brief introduction to each pillar.

The first pillar is Integrity. The definition of integrity

that I would like to work with in this book is based in ontology, which is the study of the nature of being. In ontology, *who* you are *being* is more important than *what* you are *doing*. If you are being resentful while doing a 'nice' thing because you feel obligated, the energy of that action will be resentful and inauthentic. If you are honest with yourself, you can tell when this is the case, and you can pick it up in others as well. Our energy always precedes our words and actions, and because we are all connected, our energy is picked up telepathically, without formal communication.

Therefore, the way you live is always more important than what you do. If you aren't going to do something with integrity, I suggest you wait to, or don't do it at all. That being said, the definition of integrity is doing what you know to do, when you know to do it, the way you know it is meant to be done.

Simple, right? We wish. Too often, we procrastinate in getting the work done that we know needs to get done. We even procrastinate on the things that we *want* to do. Why? Because we are out of integrity and do not know it.

When you buy a new car, everything is in integrity. It runs how it is supposed to run, when it is supposed to run. As the days, weeks, and months go by, there is regular maintenance to keep up with, for example, the tires. As the miles go up, the tires go bald. With each rotation, the tires get more and more out of integrity. As they get thinner, they don't work as well as they used to. They don't do this on purpose. They aren't lazy or entitled tires. They are just doing their job over and over again and wear out naturally. Same with all the other maintenance of the car. By way of being a car, it needs care, attention, and maintenance.

I love using this example, because when we apply our humanness, we apply judgment. When you are in your life, using your body, mind, and soul, you also require care, attention, and maintenance. You have physical, mental, emotional, and spiritual needs that you must tend to and keep up with. Failing to do so results in an inability to perform your duties that you know to do, when you know to do them, the way you know they are meant to be done.

It is our lack of self-care that throws our integrity out of whack. If you were well cared for, nourished, hydrated, well-rested, and clear, you would have nothing left to do than strive for excellence in everything that you do. If you were healthy, wealthy, and at peace, of course you would be operating at peak performance. If you were fully in love with yourself, you would be treating your mind, body, and soul like that shiny, brand new car, and taking great care of it to keep it running smoothly. The same goes for your life.

If you stay in integrity, you will discover that so many elements of your life will run smoothly and successfully. If you were operating with integrity constantly, an unexpected breakdown would be nothing more than a chance to get back into integrity. If integrity were your priority, anything to distract you from it would seem small and insignificant.

This pillar isn't magic, it's integrity.

The next pillar is Alignment. I love this pillar. It has a bit more magic to it. Alignment is the second pillar because it sits at the corner where integrity and faith meet. Alignment is the combination of clarity and energy.

When I work with a client and they are empowered to become their highest and best self, Alignment becomes a non-negotiable factor. Once we have worked through Self Discovery and shift into Self Development, I often have them write a one, three, five, ten, and twenty year plan. This is important, because once you are ready to step up as the creator of your life experience; you have to get really clear about what it is you are creating.

Listen, love. Vague goals equal vague results. If you are unclear or half clear about what you want, you will get little or half of what you are hoping for. When you discover exactly how powerful you are, you will learn to speak up when putting your order in with the Universe. God can't wait to give you all that you are asking for, but you are going to have to come from the soul and say it with your heart when you start making declarations.

Alignment is a crucial pillar, because we are constantly uncovering more of our fullest lives every day. We are faced with literally thousands of decisions daily, and what we choose has an impact on the direction and trajectory of our lives. Because of this, we will be faced with countless choices to make, and we must be clear and aligned to go after what we desire.

Endless streams of options, invitations, and temptations will come to us daily. Being in alignment with our vision affords us the fortitude to choose only what is in service of our highest good. This also gives us the power and peace to pass on tempting opportunities to get off track and out of integrity.

Being in alignment helps judgment roll right off your back when someone, or your inner critic, begins to chatter with doubt, rejection, or criticism about your choices. No one knows your fullest vision but you. Sometimes, not even you have the fullest vision. God, your Guardian Angels, Ancestors, and Spirit Guides can see much further down the path than you can. When you get distracted by self-judgment for not being where you expect to be in life, that is the perfect time to rely on the alignment you have with your Higher Power.

This is exactly where the third pillar, Faith, comes into play. Practicing faith in the unseen, unheard, and unknown will propel you into abundance you could not possibly imagine. In my own times of judgment or weakness I hear God's whisper, "Not a moment sooner, child. If only you knew the things I have planned for you." In these moments, I wipe my tears and pray for faith to help me get back into alignment and integrity.

Faith is a pillar that is usually the weakest when I first meet clients, because their Earth experience and religion has tainted their connection with the Divine. When I say weakest, I mean crumbling like a cookie. I will support you in strengthening this pillar in a way that increases your faith in the greatness of God. When you heal and recreate this relationship, it will recreate your life.

I will openly share with you that judgment could have easily stopped me from not writing this section, or even this book. My concern of catering to everyone's belief systems has me second guessing my use of God's name. I could have given in, watered it down, and rewritten it for fear of saying something 'incorrect' or losing you to the "eh, I'm not with the whole God thing." Trust me, I wrote all about quitting religion in my first book. It took me two to three decades to recreate my relationship with God. I request you give me two to three chapters in the Faith pillar to help you make that shift, too.

As you may be able to tell, the Faith I am referring to as a pillar is not about attending church or making weekly donations. The God I am referring to isn't some white-haired man in the sky, keeping score of your sins for when you arrive to your judgment day. This is about the deepest level of connection with the God Source Energy within you, that guides you to live in the purest love this Universe has to offer.

Finding your faith is about tapping into that wellspring of abundance that fuels your life to the fullest. Beyond your own life, this is about bringing the presence of God into the lives of others and walking them home. When these three pillars are strong for you, every interaction will be a holy interaction. You will transcend judgment as you come to understand that every single thing is an expression of the Universe experiencing itself. Ultimately, this is a training manual for compassion. It is simultaneously a challenge and invitation to connect to everything and every being as an extension of you. Let that excite you as you imagine how playful life can be.

When you are operating in Integrity, Alignment, and Faith, you will experience all of the room in the world to dance, play, create, explore, expand, and enjoy. You will be a light for others and rewarded handsomely. You will be fulfilled and hilariously joyful. I want that for you, and my guess is you want that, too.

It is very possible, and I will teach you exactly how to win this game we call life.

Integrity Pillar

Chapter 4

Judgment

Welp, let's get right down to the topic at hand: judgment. Judgment is the root of negative emotions. It comes in all shapes and sizes, such as rejection, guilt, shame, anger, envy, frustration, resentment, pride, hatred, and more.

When this book came to me, *it* told *me* its name. I heard it loud and clear one day and wrote it down. I knew exactly what it would be about because in my coaching career I have seen thousands of ways that judgment can manifest. I will use examples throughout this book, and I mean it when I say that the possibilities are endless. Judgment shapeshifts and morphs into different identities. It is so shifty, that when you think you have solved it or have rid yourself of it, it will rear its ugly head some other way.

As I shared earlier, you must surrender any and all attempts to eradicate judgment, and instead accept it fully. Judgment can completely run your life if you do not acknowledge, face, and reformulate it. Beyond accepting it, I am asking you to study it. Learn it so well that you can recognize it comin' a mile down the pipe.

To transcend judgment simply means to master it in a way that you are not unconsciously operating by it. When you cannot see it, it runs you from the inside out, and then the outside in. Similar to how a fish doesn't recognize water, and we hardly recognize the air; we exist in judgment so naturally that we hardly recognize how much we function by it. You project your judgments on to the world outside of yourself constantly, and you see it reflected back everywhere. This pattern will keep solidifying your beliefs, making it hard to see them for what they are and rise above them. While this isn't always bad, it can be limiting in so many ways. Being able to identify this occurrence will allow you to work with it and transcend judgment.

I want to take you even deeper down the rabbit hole, past judgment, to see what it really is: separation.

Separation is an illusion that allows us to judge. Feeling separate from something grants us permission to evaluate it as if it is not us. I can practically hear your inner voice arguing, "Nu-uh, Abby! I judge myself more than others! I am my toughest critic!" I get that.

You even have to separate yourself from yourself, in order to judge yourself. You judge your body as if it is not yours. You reject your skin and hair when it doesn't do what you want it to do. You judge your hips for carrying more weight than you want. You judge your organs, bones, or joints when they aren't performing the way you hope or expect. You judge your brain for being dumb or stubborn and your heart for being weak. You may think you are judging yourself, but you are splitting yourself to do so.

You separate yourself from other individuals, places, things, and situations in order to be able to judge them. This is the only way you can judge, because then you aren't required to take meaningful responsibility for addressing the issue at hand and getting it back into integrity and alignment.

To judge is to reject. To judge is to maintain distance between you and that which you judge. You do this so you can avoid the feeling of inadequacy you so deeply fear. In order to project inadequacy onto someone or something else, you must create the illusion of separation in your mind to validate your judgment. When you judge someone or something, you believe it to be above or below you in the hierarchy. You feel that inadequacy within yourself and it triggers resentment, envy, and more.

Some inadequacies include: not good enough, too much, unlovable, fundamentally flawed, rotten, damaged, perverted, deranged, demonic, faulty, etc. We harbor these thoughts about ourselves at the subconscious level, and sometimes, they surface to our conscious mind as well. If we are emotionally undeveloped and cannot be with these thoughts and feelings, we will numb out, check out, distract, avoid, and project. I talk all about the ways we numb out, check out, distract, and avoid in my fourth book, titled *I Can't: The Greatest Lie in Human History*.

In this book, we will focus on the projections of judgment and how to shift the behavior of putting judgment out into the Universe. I will teach you how to emanate much higher ratios of love than judgment, because remember; we cannot truly rid it. It *will* bounce back. We can learn to alchemize it in such a way that we are getting love, light, and opportunities from it, instead.

For a powerful visual, recall how I said judgment is the core of negative emotions. Imagine judgment as being the trunk of a large tree. Each branch is a different form of judgment, such as rejection, guilt, shame, anger, envy, frustration, resentment, pride, hatred, and more. Each branch grows twigs, leaves, blossoms, and bears fruit. Then, that fruit ripens, falls off, and rots at the base of the tree. You have the fruits of your judgment rotting at the base of your life and this fruit is falling everywhere. It is your responsibility to clean it up and stop the cycle.

If judgment is the trunk, then separation is the roots. You root yourself in the illusion of separation and give your judgment a firm foundation upon which to grow and manifest. The ripened and rotting fruit nourishes the ground and re-feeds the roots the same energy from that which it came, therefore, keeping that tree alive and strong.

We must starve this tree, deny it nourishment, and uproot it. We must stop the fruit from growing and falling, thus stopping the cycle. This can be a bit harsh, like going on a diet and then having intense cravings from the sudden denial. Although that may be an effective strategy physically speaking, mentally, we must keep the end game in mind; to starve the judgment tree to its withering death.

Just kidding. We are not killing judgment. Remember, *we can't!* Don't you get it yet?! For as long as you are human, you will have judgments. I will keep making that clear throughout this book, because you already have decade's worth of judgmental patterns, and those are the fuel for your growth. I am simply helping you evolve those patterns to empower yourself and those around you.

Listen, my friend. These judgments are so deeply ingrained in the blueprint of your being, that they will always exist as tools in your toolbox. I want you to prepare yourself to use your tools to build, not destroy.

So, oddly enough, I am going to teach you how to tend to your judgment tree, so that it is healthy and thriving! Keep in mind, tending to it doesn't turn it into something else. You cannot turn an apple tree into an orange tree. You cannot turn the judgment tree into a love tree. You can just catch the fruit before they rot and make jam.

Keep in mind that there are judgments that are healthy. 'Jumping from heights is unsafe,' or 'spending all my money with this salesman doesn't feel right,' are good judgments as well as forms of guidance from your intuition to think before you act. To manicure your judgment tree will have you discerning between judgments that serve you and those that do not.

What this looks like when tending to your judgment

tree would be picking up the old fruit, picking off the ripe fruit, and cutting down dead branches. As you can imagine, in life this looks like ending toxic habits and relationships. This looks like setting boundaries and learning how to say "No" as a one word sentence. These are some examples of integrity, which we will continue to cover in later chapters.

Beyond clean up, you must familiarize yourself with the branches that remain. You can better understand the branches of your judgment tree by drawing a picture of it, or by writing down what they consist of in list form. For the best inventory, list until you can't list anymore. Then, for a few days in a row, go back and add more to ensure you don't miss any of the ways you judge.

By doing this, you will likely be able to identify which are branches and which are twigs. For example, the envy branch could include jealousy, gossip, cheating, stealing, betrayal, and other acts of envy. The twigs are actions, the leaves are thoughts, the blossoms are words, and the fruit is well, the fruit. Your words, thoughts, and actions bear fruit in your life.

As explained previously, the fruits of your thoughts, feelings, words, and actions manifest physically in your reality to reflect the energy you are putting out. This might look like bad health, deteriorating relationships, bouts of bad luck, financial hardship, low self-esteem, mental and emotional illness, etc. This seemingly natural momentum of negativity can be turned around with the tending of your overgrown judgment tree. The quality and direction of your life are one hundred percent reliant upon this understanding. Transmute your emotions, thoughts, words, and actions; transform your life.

Once you have identified all of the branches, it is time to start chopping and trimming. Gossip, stealing, substance abuse, lying, harming, promiscuity, littering, and eating poorly do not serve you in any way. They don't serve the people around you, or this planet. These are just a few examples of what can be cut out. It is up to you to identify and decide what goes first, and just chop, chop, chop away.

The order doesn't matter, and I encourage my clients to start small and get good at chopping a small branch before moving on too quickly. If we move too rapidly, we can get sloppy and go back to old patterns without even knowing we're doing it. Just keep in mind that the more you do it, the more you do it. Over time and repetition, you become better at releasing disempowering thoughts, habits, and patterns. You must stay aware, responsible, and hold yourself accountable to do this work over and over again.

So in case it isn't obvious, I want to remind you of how nature works. What does a tree do? That's right, it grows. The branches, twigs, and leaves *will* grow back if you do not tend to your tree frequently. Don't get too exhausted by the thought of this. It takes diligence, but maintenance is nowhere near as daunting as the initial clean-up. This looks like living a conscious and mindful life. It looks like mediation, journaling, and prayer. It is simply a diligent effort to live from your heart space, which I will teach you to do in the Alignment portion of this book.

As for the rest of this section, I will be breaking down the various components of integrity so that you have the necessary tools to take full responsibility for your judgment and maintain your light in the presence of darkness. I will explain the mechanics of concepts that you know of but may not fully understand. I will even introduce a few new-to-you concepts, or ones that you have not associated with integrity. This section will effectively reflect your judgment only if you are willing to practice maturity and responsibility for yourself, your life, and your impact. This is an opportunity to witness your judgement in action but will require your willingness to see.

As you continue on, notice any resistance or justifying that comes up, and practice opening up your heart space to receive this information fully. You are reading this book to learn. When you get triggered or annoyed, pause your reading, close your eyes, relax your shoulders, and breathe deeply until you feel back in your body and ready to receive more information and guidance.

Practicing these skills throughout the duration of this book will also help you with their practical application. This means that when you notice you are judging, justifying, and separating in real life, you can use these lessons then, as well. I am excited to begin this journey of transformation with you.

Chapter 5

Projection

If you think about a projector machine, you understand that it shines an image from the inside of it onto something outside of it. You do this with your mind all day, every day. The image in your mind forms the visions you see in the world.

If you believe all men are pigs in your mind, you will see this image projected into your reality. If you believe that everyone is out for your money, you will see freeloaders everywhere. If you believe that people are helpless, entitled, and selfish, you will attract exactly those kinds of people, and feel constantly taken advantage of and exhausted by it. If you tell yourself that you are unlovable, the world will show you all sorts of reasons why, and you will collect evidence of it to reinforce that belief.

You project your beliefs constantly, and do you know where your beliefs come from? Your past.

You are never looking at this world for what it is.

You are looking at this world for how you see, or *have* seen it. You are projecting your past into your future and it's all you can see in your present. This can be confusing when others don't see the world the way you do.

"How can she land a man and I can't? How did he make it to the top so easily? Of course he's rich, he's got more going for him." We judge and justify all day long without taking responsibility for the beliefs we are projecting from within.

We don't know the stories of how she bagged the man, he got the job, or made all the money. We don't know the struggle they endured or the strength required to have arrived where they did. We are just projecting our single experience of the world onto others as if *our* version of the world is *the* version of the world.

This is separation in action. We stay in our singular perspectives without considering alternative options or possibilities and stay stagnant in judgment. Since I assume you would rather not live this way, I am going to start dissecting projection so you can choose alternative ways of being.

Let's start by recalling that this universe is a giant, mirrored room. What you put out, you get back. Said my favorite way; as within, so without. As above, so below. This is a subtle, yet obvious gauge for how someone is doing internally. The state of someone's car, bedroom, office, relationships, health, and finances are often a direct reflection of their internal state. Even those who are making great progress in their life can then catch themselves experiencing breakdowns if their physical environment is getting out of whack, or as I will explain in this first pillar: out of integrity.

Messy room, messy mind. Aching body, struggling soul. Broken relationships, broken heart. This can vary on the scale or severity but to stay aware of this knowledge will help you keep yourself in check along the path of transformation. We all need to stay actively involved in our state of affairs to experience being at choice about our life. When we loosen up on this, things unravel and we can't quite figure out why we feel out of whack again.

Everything in your life is a projection of what is going on within you. If you can see this and accept it, you can start cleaning up your head and heart space and your life will follow suit. Many people convince themselves it occurs the other way around, and this lie keeps them in patterns of starting diets, half reading personal development books, paying for a gym membership they don't use, and buying quick-fix gadgets off of infomercials.

Many think that if they could finally lose the weight, then they would be happy. The problem with that idea is that the weight is a reflection of worthlessness, self-hate, undeservedness, and more. Others convince themselves that having money will help them feel successful. I love money as much as the next gal and I am here to tell you that money vibrates at a high frequency. Raise your frequency, raise the balance in your bank account. It is hard to make more money when you're wallowing in self-pity. It is time to start accepting that outer work doesn't fix the inner work. Inner work causes the outer manifestation. As that cycle repeats, it creates an upward spiral that results in a more natural inspiration to live a great life.

I love when 'all of a sudden' my clients can't stand the mess they are living in and start purging, cleaning, and rearranging. After a few weeks of working together, they practically snap out of a daze and start to see the mess around them. This leads to what I call an 'integrity rampage' which I will explain later in this book.

In short, the integrity rampage happens after folks begin cleaning up their head and heart space. They no longer have certain images running in their minds; therefore, they are no longer projecting that image in their life. Like a fog lifts on a dewy morning, things come into plain view and look different than ever before. Suddenly, the dishes need to be washed and the laundry put away. The car must be vacuumed, the tank full, and the cup holders cleaned.

The integrity rampage can happen serendipitously, too. People lose a job they never liked but wouldn't quit. Significant others break up with us before we manage to break up with them. The doctor tells you that you have three months to live. When we begin transformation, things are miraculously moved out of our way to clear our path.

Without the awareness that some integrity and realignment is 'forced' upon us serendipitously, we can become too distracted by the losses and see them as failures, punishments, or signs to stop. We miss seeing that these are our own projections of our deepest sub-conscious desires manifesting to shift us. We don't realize that we are being redirected by a Higher Power that also has a higher perspective than we do. When the Universe clears your path, trust it. See the invitation to move forward for what it is and take the next step toward improving your future.

This is important to understand as we dive deeper into understanding projection because we are going to make this personal now. In terms of separation, we try to make the problems in our life about others. We point, blame, and shame. We make endless excuses about why things are the way they are, and why we can't catch a break. The next chapter is about accountability and responsibility, but before we go there, we must see exactly what there is to take responsibility for.

A few hard truths about judgment:

- A judgment of another is a judgment of yourself.
- If you can spot something in someone, you have it too.
- What you judge in others is something you cannot see, refuse to accept, or fear about yourself.
- You judge what you are afraid of or don't understand.
- You judge that which you wish you had the courage to be, do, or have.

It is one of my favorite exercises to listen to some-one rag on another and when they are all done, I hold up a mirror to them and ask them to repeat everything they said. Almost immediately, the tears start streaming.

When we swap 'they' for 'I' it becomes obvious why that person would be showing up in our lives and challenging us the way they are. Almost immediately, a person can see in themselves what they are judging in that other person. This is where real transformation occurs. It is not in judgment, but rather, in the opportunity to see a part of us that has gone unseen. It is a direct invitation to transmute hate and rejection into clarity, understanding, love, and acceptance.

People come into our lives to reflect us so that we may see ourselves. You may not be ready to be honest with yourself about that, and that is okay. It doesn't change the mechanics of this equation. Whenever you become ready, write down all your judgments of someone and sit in front of a mirror to read them aloud. In order to make a true and lasting shift, you must be able to identify that judgment within you, even if that part of you is just the size of a grain of sand.

You know who calls people narcissists? You know who calls people selfish? You know who calls people lazy? You guessed it. Lazy, selfish, narcissists.

Now, before you toss this book out the window, take a deep breath and open your heart. People come into your life to reflect these things *so that* you can handle them. We are given people to empower our decision to *not* be that way and have that impact on others. We get the gift of these challenges in our lives so we can tend to the judgment tree and trim some branches. Growing up as a human, we all have so many of these dark characteristics. It is in our intentional choice to live consciously so that we are afforded the opportunity to transcend these ways of being. It is possible. Just don't throw this book out of the window before you get to the good part.

I once had a client who understood this reflection concept so well. She would message me a complaint about her husband knowing that I would simply ask her how she is embodying the traits that she is complaining about. She got so good at this that she would humbly reply "ahhhhh, got it. Thanks." And go back about her day. This doesn't need to be a moral debacle; it is as simple as awareness and acceptance. To accept your judgments and behaviors is to also take your power back from them. Acceptance is the process of alchemizing judgment.

Speaking of complaining about others, do you want to know who annoys me? Loud, obnoxious, attention seekers. Crazy, right? Because I have none of those traits...

When we are annoyed by aspects of someone, we must look for them in ourselves. Sometimes, we are not aware of our ways until we see them in others. They can be easily identified by that "ew" feeling. When someone seems repulsive, they are reflecting a part of ourselves that we feel repulsed by. Usually, this is a part of us that we try to cover up with make-up, money, achievements, attention, and more. As long as we reject the parts of us, we don't like, our projector machine will flash them all over our lives. It is not a curse, but an invitation to see our whole selves. It is truly a gift to witness our totality.

Accepting every part of ourselves is what helps transform the projections of our minds. I will expound upon this topic more in the Alignment Pillar chapter.

Before we can get into alignment, we must practice willingness to understand the things that we don't understand. We judge situations that seem weird, different, wrong, bad, grotesque, and perverted, because we want to be able to keep those feelings at a comfortable distance from us. We do not want to associate with certain things and let me tell you my friend: what you resist persists.

This book is about alchemizing judgment, not getting rid of it. You cannot rid it. You cannot rid the world of people you don't like. You cannot rid the Earth of bugs. You cannot rid the sky of clouds. You must alchemize your feelings about those things lest they steal all of your power, joy, and choice. For each of us, the objects that our judgment is focused on will vary. Judgment is subjective. Therefore, we must recognize that judgment is not right, wrong, good, or bad; it is relative. The way we don't like a rainy day is relative to thinking clouds and rain equate 'bad' or 'sad.' The way I don't like a spider in my house is relative to believing they belong outside. These statements are not necessarily true or false, they are relative.

Judgments are natural. They are associations. To transcend your associations means you recognize they are specific to your world view and that you make up rules, standards, boundaries, and expectations to match them. This does not make them true or relative to anyone else. Your beliefs are yours and they are your responsibility, but if we simply project our prejudices based on our beliefs, we will be forced to look at them more closely.

If you understand the Law of Attraction, to reject what you don't like or understand will draw it closer and closer to you until you become willing to examine it. The more you resist, the closer it will get. Do not tempt this theory, because it will get so close to you that it will literally enter your body as illness and disease.

The Law of Attraction is not all sunshine and rainbows of "what you think about you bring about." It is the beliefs and images of your subconscious that get projected, not just your conscious mantras and desires. Your subconscious projects because that is the only way it can communicate with you. It speaks in manifestations, internally and externally. You must become willing to slow down and witness the manifestations to receive their communications.

These projections will give you a chance to shift the deepest, darkest corners of your heart and mind. This will provide you an opportunity to shed light in dark spaces and transmute what lingers there. For example, harboring resentment for your upbringing will fester in your energetic body as hatred and anger. This *may* be directed at your parents, and it will also disproportionately come out in other relationships, at work, toward yourself, and your circumstances.

Your anger will consume you and run your life. Your projection will be seen through a filter of anger.

Like wearing a pair of red glasses, everything will be tinted with rage, and you will always be a hairline away from a full-blown meltdown. This might also manifest as headaches, stomachaches, cancer, intrusive thoughts, mental illness, bipolar disorders, substance abuse, sexual addictions, frivolous spending, and more.

I am teaching you all of this not to condemn or diagnose you, but rather, to give you choice in the matter. Not one single emotion is permanent. Even your past is not permanent the way you think it is. In the next chapter, I will teach you about reframing. This tactic will help you create a new relationship with your memories so that you may shift the emotions caused by them. This will transmute the memory's energy, allowing yourself a release from the clutches of your past.

When you do this, your projections begin to shift, as well. Instead of past projecting, you are giving yourself a clean, blank slate from which to imagine and create your future from a more authentic place.

One of the last ways we judge others is through envy. We see others who understand these lessons already, have done the work of putting their past in the past, have cleared their head and heart, and are now creating a life they love. These people live freely, laugh loudly, and love intensely. We watch these folks dance, sing, play, travel, spend, and exist without limitations... and it drives us wild. We scoff and scowl at their freedom and fortune. Sometimes, we even convince ourselves that we could care less. We pretend like we don't want what they seem to attain so easily.

For me, I used to judge women harshly who wore revealing clothing. Meanwhile, I would also stare in jealousy at their beautiful bodies, wishing I had that confidence. I knew that if I felt that confident about my legs or belly, I would wear that, too.

I also knew that my inner dialogue wasn't my own. It was a voice I call 'Catholic Guilt,' that critiqued these women for allowing their bodies to be seen. Before I started allowing myself to wear what I want, I remember the shame I experienced about feeling sexy and being in love with my body in my twenties. The voice of Catholic Guilt kept me in line for a long time and also kept me feeling jealous of women who didn't seem to have that voice in their heads. They seemed to have freedom, and I was certainly jealous of that.

I am sure we can all recall a time in which we have judged someone solely because they had the confidence, power, and poise that we wish we had for ourselves. We also judge people's relationships and possessions for this same exact reason. We covet our neighbor's goods because we wish we felt deserving enough to have those same blessings in our lives. We might also covet because we feel denied or at a loss for why we are not succeeding in ways we hoped or planned to.

When it comes to judgment; if you didn't covet it, you wouldn't judge it. Of course, we're not always coveting. We can be genuinely happy for people's blessings without attachment, and it is also helpful to notice when you are not genuinely celebrating someone's wins and successes. If a sense of envy or longing gets activated within you in these moments, it is a great opportunity to better understand yourself.

You don't judge your neighbor's front door wreath if you have no desire for a front door wreath, but you may judge the size of their house. You do not want your sister's hairbrush as much as you want the thriving relationship she has. You don't spend energy thinking about your boss' laptop as much as you do having their position or salary.

Coveting someone else's something is a signal from your subconscious that it is time to do some inner work. It's a sign of something missing or incomplete within you, and you have the power to heal that with some intentional introspection. This is the work of recognizing and alchemizing judgment. This is transcending your humanness.

Envy can fool us and keep us locked in place. If we spend more time judging others than evaluating our judgment, we will remain in that mindset, and never have access to peace, contentment, or abundance. I want you to know that there is hope and light at the end of the judgment tunnel.

This chapter is specifically committed to simply recognizing your judgments. Be sure to take a few deep breaths before moving onto the next chapter, where I will teach you how to take responsibility and accountability for these judgments. This can be heavy and intense, because I am asking you to be more honest with yourself than normal. I am asking you to see parts of yourself that you have become good at stuffing and avoiding.

Relax your face, neck, and shoulders as you take three, really deep inhales that bring fresh air all the way into your body. Then, push out judgment on your exhales. I hope that you have discovered a lot in this chapter, and I acknowledge you for making it to this point. Soften your body as you begin to practice new levels of self-acceptance for the ways you have consciously and subconsciously judged. If you are really committed to this process, after your three deep breath cycles, announce out loud "I forgive myself" three times in a row, and again, focus on relaxing your body.

Great work, my friend. Let's keep going.

Chapter 6

Responsibility & Accountability

We have taken two really crucial steps in this process and they were big ones. Understanding judgment and projection are whopper-sized lessons and I commend your expansion. Can you sense yourself becoming an alchemist yet? I am going to keep diving deeper into the work and it will likely keep stretching you. I want to shine a light from the end of the tunnel to tell you that the Integrity Pillar is the heavy lifting in this book.

We are working on removing gunk that has been around for years, and so, naturally, it might feel like a lot of exhausting work. I want to reassure you that you are doing great. Because you are doing decades' worth of work, this book may feel like a lot to take on in one read. That is okay and a natural feeling if it is what you are experiencing. Do not be tough on yourself if you feel like it is too much, too soon. This is a *guidebook* in the sense that you may reference it time and time again to return to the work when you need a refresher. Take what you can and leave what feels like too much for a later read. This is life-changing work, my love, and you are doing great. Let's keep going and growing.

We have been uncovering a lot of information so far and this chapter is all about working with your new awareness. It is about shifting from knowledge to wisdom. What you know doesn't serve you. Repeat after me: "what I know doesn't serve me."

You can memorize and recite the entire dictionary and never apply that knowledge to your life, because there is a difference between what you know in your head and what you own in your heart. To internalize these lessons of this book within yourself is what makes them your truth. To shift from intellect to ownership will transform you from a student to a teacher. This is your responsibility in life. You do not have to accept this obligation but remember, this guidebook is to help you thrive.

To make that task more inviting, I have promised to take the complexity out of the mysterious concept of alchemy. I feel called to do this for those of you who are like me. The ones committed to this task, and equally baffled by the process. I remember certain leaders simply encouraging the work and not offering guidance through the journey. I remember feeling so lost, confused, frustrated, and alone at certain stages of my transformation because of this. I am determined to provide you the support I was seeking, and I am committed to walking this journey with you. So, I am laying this out for you, step, by ever-loving step.

When reviewing this book, my editor, Val, asked me about the order of the pillars. I explained to her how this was the first book I had ever written in chapter order; word by word, page by page, trying to have my fingers keep up with the streams of consciousness flowing like whitewater rapids. It was a phenomenal experience that stretched me as a writer and leader in ways that I imagine it will similarly stretch you as a reader. Walk the path in faith, allow yourself to be led through this book, and I promise to keep dropping breadcrumbs of guidance along the way. As you make your way through each chapter, your load will lighten. Each chapter is designed to help you drop mental and emotional weight and have you floating, maybe even soaring, by the end of it.

This is a chapter all about responsibility, accountability, and application, as well as a big instructional step in transformation. I value this upcoming material greatly, because it has so much to do with my own sense of purpose; unleashing hearts so that you may live out your authentic leadership in this world. It is about seeing and accepting that you have an impact on this world. It is not a matter of *if*. It is a matter of *how*.

Think of five very different people you know and notice the impact they have on your life. Think about the energy they bring into the room and how your body feels around them. Think about what thoughts you think in their presence and what you are left with after they leave. Think about the ways that each person influences your feelings about yourself, others, and the world. Notice how your energetic experience shifts when thinking about each of the five individuals.

This is impactful. You have impact. You must become aware of this if you are going to become an alchemist. If you desire to transmute any and all energy back into love, you must become hyperaware of the energy you naturally emanate. You must become one hundred percent responsible for your impact.

You cannot shift that which you cannot see. Therefore, you must become aware of your impact before you can elevate it. One effective way of doing this is to consider all of the things that I just invited you to consider about others, and instead consider them in reference to yourself. You can consider these components on your own or take some time to ask other people about your impact. You will, of course, get a variety of answers, and you will see some patterns as well. This is a healthy exercise in seeing yourself outside of your own projections.

To find out that you talk about yourself more than you listen to others, and that it is draining for those around you, can actually cause you to choose a new way of being. Your discovery that you seem emotionally unavailable can become an invitation to open up and express yourself more. To unveil that others feel safe and comfortable around your grounding calmness can encourage you to be that way with more intention and commitment.

Awareness is a powerful tool that gives us choice. You can choose your way of being. You can choose what you put out into the Universe. You can choose your impact and when you are doing that, you are choosing to receive greater blessings in return.

Think of yourself as an electronic device. You are sending out waves and signals that cannot be seen by the naked eye, but they can be sensed by the heart. Humans, animals, plants, and even the elements can sense your energy and are affected by it. This is your impact on the planet. You can imagine the ripple effect of your frequency. This is why it is utterly important you take responsibility for your energy.

Imagine someone you know who vibrates at a low frequency. They are negative, pessimistic, rude, and crass. They scowl and shrug and grunt. You can feel judgment seeping from their being and it causes a physical response in you. You can feel their heavy energy pushing down on your shoulders. You feel a tightening of your neck and chest. Your ears and cheeks get warm and your gag reflex becomes activated. This is Impact.

When we are sloppy, lazy, and irresponsible with our impact, we cause a negative ripple effect around us. We bring others down, and others bring others down. I call this the Cycle of Harm.

Let's say you wake up late, barely have time to get ready, and rush out of the door for work, unprepared. Then, in your rush, you drive recklessly, nearly running someone off the road. That has an impact and you may be too rushed to even realize it. They, in turn, react, and feel irritated. That person then stops at the gas station and gives the cashier a bad attitude. This makes the cashier perturbed, who becomes short tempered with the next customer. Let's say the customer is a father, filling up before taking the kids to school. The dad, now angry, gets back in the car and yells at the kids to turn off the loud music, and the kids become hushed and upset. Arriving at school upset, the oldest brother treats a classmate aggressively. The classmate comes home crying to their mom, the mom reacts, and the story goes on, and on, and on. The ripple effect rolls on, and on, and on.

This cycle can most definitely occur in the opposite direction, as what I like to call: the Cycle of Love. You can still wake up late and intentionally commit to maintaining your calmness. With great, new skills learned in this book, you can choose the impact you want to have and get grounded before charging into your day at full…or foolish…speed.

You can ground, breathe, and reset, allowing you to get back to being in a state of love by processing your feelings of disappointment, self-frustration, and urgency. Believe it or not, you can accomplish this before your feet ever hit the ground. You can forgive yourself for missing your alarm clock and grant yourself permission to be late to where you are going. You can get into communication with anyone affected by your tardiness and inform them about your new time of arrival. All of this will grant you an opportunity to get fully ready for the day, without running out of your own body or forgetting your impact on others.

Nothing is that important. What we prioritize as

important is a projection of our beliefs. If you had different beliefs, you would have different priorities, as everyone does. Nothing is so important that you cannot get your wits about you before proceeding onward. This awareness and ability will completely transform the pace, direction, and experience of your life.

The Cycles of Harm and Love can be direct, like the examples I shared, and they can be indirect. I try to watch the world in slow motion. I move with intention and am conscious of my impact. I understand that I share this world with seven billion people, and I respect the coexistence. This awareness is a large factor in my commitment to being a contributing member of humanity, instead of operating as if humanity functions in response to me. This influences how I exist in public, in private, and in service to others. It even inspires my desire to lessen my carbon footprint; I do my best to use less harmful products, create less waste, and consume less as to not cause more harm to the planet and humanity.

Indirectly, maintaining your peace is a contribution to the Collective. By being one less person *not* contributing to the Cycle of Harm, you are helping slow the negative momentum.

Besides that, you are turning the tide from negative to positive. It can be so simple. It is *meant* to be so simple. Waving to someone results in a smile. A hug or a smile passed on might cause a compliment or act of kindness. The small stuff can add up to make a big difference, but the small stuff overlooked can cause a big problem. By staying conscious and intentional, you are contributing to the acceleration of a positive ripple to spread far and wide.

Taking responsibility for your impact is vital to our species' success, and in order for it to have a real effect, everyone must play their role. This knowledge is not intended for you to fix or change others' impact. This information is to allow you to take one hundred percent responsibility for your own. If you hold yourself accountable for your impact, you will inspire others to become more conscious and accountable for their own. In due time, it is likely that people who witness your light will seek your guidance about effectively harnessing and directing their energy for the highest good of all. You will not have to force your hand at this. You will simply have to practice this discipline for yourself. More is caught than taught when it comes to impact, and your actions will always speak louder than your words.

Speaking of words, let's talk about the sheer power and impact of language. You may sense that I am discussing the power of language quite seriously, and this is because of how powerful I understand language to be. I am the most rigorous with my clients and students about language because I can see them painting the picture of their life with their conversations. Your words create your world.

As mentioned in the previous chapter, you may not be ready to take responsibility for your language, but it doesn't change the equation. Your words create your world. Being sloppy or irresponsible with your words is detrimental to your progress in transformation. Taking accountability for your language is one of *the* most important tasks you can take on to directly improve your life. To ignore this simply slows you down or sabotages your efforts. I encourage you to take on this work with focused commitment. I promise, you will see very direct results in relation to your consistency.

What you speak about, you bring about.

If you spew negativity out of your mouth, you will be surrounded by it. Visually, imagine standing in a pool full of your words and conversations. How does that feel? If you know you wouldn't like that experience, it is time to become conscious of and responsible for your language.

- Life is hard.
- Money is fleeting.
- I'm such an idiot.
- I hate my…
- It will never get better.
- This is how I am.
- That is just the way it is.

Self-deprecation, harsh criticisms, pessimistic projecting, complaining, gossiping, or withholding are all a hindrance. They vibrate at a low frequency, similar to scowling, scoffing, and shrugging.

Recall the judgment tree. Words are blossoms that bloom on the branches of judgment. They grow from thoughts and feelings in accordance with the judgment. Therefore, in order to shift your language, you must first alchemize the deeply rooted judgment back to love. As a natural byproduct, your language will shift to reflect your internal state. This fuels the upwards spiral of empowering manifestations that inspire integrity, alignment, and faith. It doesn't start outside of you. It begins within.

That doesn't mean that you should wait for your internal state to completely alter before becoming more responsible for your language. I am incredibly rigorous about my client's language in ways that shift who and how they are, from the inside out.

For example: I am a hawk about the uses of 'need to, have to, gotta, should, supposed to' language. I am committed to helping people understand that they don't *have* to do anything. Will there be consequences for not doing certain things? Of course, but I make my clients consider themselves at choice about every single thing in their lives. I will go into depth about being at choice later. For now, I challenge you to become much more intentional about your word selection. If you are curious about this specific example, I encourage you to start using 'get to, want to, intend to, and choose to' when talking about what you are doing in life.

This is an example of present tense reframing. To reframe how you relate to something reframes your attitude and shifts your way of being. Putting yourself at choice shifts you from being a victim of obligation, to a leader of life. As promised in the last chapter, I will explain how to reframe your past in a way that helps you release it, and therefore prevent it from adding more mental and emotional weight.

You came here to live. So far, you have lived. Going forward, you will continue to live. By definition of living, you will have experiences and they will create more memories. That collection of memories will be what you consider your past. Some of those memories will have more energy and impact and will likely replay in your mind, seeming more like the present than the past.

This happens because these are moments in time in which you have learned something valuable to your existence and survival in this world. You don't remember every detail of your childhood and it is likely that the more trauma you had, the more you have naturally blocked out; more appropriately said, effectively *bottled up*. I say this because the memories still exist as energetic blocks in your nonphysical self. These occurrences in your past are when your brain has developed conclusions, and when your different survival identities and patterns were born. Blocking and bottling are not effective methods for living a thriving life. Reframing them and transmuting their energy is the only way to generate freedom.

Continuously avoiding these emotional wounds can be detrimental to your mental, emotional, and physical health. If you don't take this seriously, the consequences can be serious too. When these traumas and memories go unidentified in your body, they have the freedom to roam. I share this not to scare you, but to inspire you to appropriately acknowledge exactly how important it is to heal your wounds. Unhealed wounds are what cause intrusive thoughts, low self-esteem, crippling fear, and deep depression. Not transmuting dark energies and memories can be heavy for the mind, body, and soul, and I want to give you hope that you do not have to exist that way.

When it comes to identifying this, you may not have a specific memory of trauma at the forefront of your mind, but you may be struggling with feeling inexplicably sad, angry, anxious, and depressed. This often occurs because in our natural attempts to survive, bottling our traumas has led to confusion about the root cause of our pain. Compartmentalizing our pain separates us from it in a way that actually disempowers us. Staying in this pattern will feel like a slow leak of your power. This experience can be exhausting and defeating and can cause people to feel hopeless. It doesn't have to be this way but taking on this work will require you healing what there is to heal, even if it feels unbearable or impossible.

This is where it is so important to remember that you are not alone in this endeavor. Speaking with a professional facilitates this progress, and I will share more about this in just a few pages. Quite often, trying to do this work alone can trigger more confusion, loneliness, and hopelessness. If healing on your own worked, it would've worked by now. Again, I do not say that to scare you, I say it to implore you to plug into professional support. I ask you to be really honest with yourself in answering this question: have you done your best with what you know? Have you tried to heal alone as best as you can and still experience pain? You do not need to do this important work independently. We are not meant to do this work alone.

If you had a bullet wound, you would head to the hospital, or die ignoring it. If you had a stab wound, you would need stitches or bleed out ignoring it. If you had a scrape that got infected, you would treat it or potentially lose a limb. Would you try to perform your own surgery or stitch yourself up? Recognizing the truth in this, why is it that we ignore mental and emotional wounds? Why do we insist on healing isolated and alone?

Considering that prioritizing mental and emotional health has only recently become common, there are still millions of people walking amongst us bleeding all over the place. If you were mentally or emotionally abused, beaten, raped, neglected, or generally harmed, you can treat it or die ignoring it. Ignoring our mental and emotional wounds is the cause of illness, disease, debt, addiction, weight, self-destruction, suicide, and so on. The wounds we cannot see are more harmful than the ones we can.

Invisible wounds can walk the earth and have a negative impact everywhere they go. They bleed out in energy, actions, thoughts, feelings, and words. They could look like a perfectly healthy human with an ugly, aching heart. They might appear as a successful man who lied and forced his way through life, or a beautiful woman cheating on her husband to feel love and affection. They might even look like a teen that bullies their teammates, despite having real potential.

Our pain and suffering are subtle to us, because we

have not been taught what to look for. We have not been taught how to fully feel, nor have we been taught how to identify or communicate our needs. These are all our individual responsibilities, and yet, we don't know what we don't know. I know that I was called to write this book to contribute to this understanding and cause this shift. We must learn to recognize what is going on within us in order to alchemize our impact.

I will touch on healing our wounds in the Completion chapter coming up. Right now, I want to enroll you in the potential of what it would be like to live free of your past. Sure, our past has made us who we are, and that is great. It is important. So important, in fact, that when I hear a client tell me the life they have experienced, I can begin to understand so much about why they came to this planet and what they are here to do. I hear them speaking their purpose and leadership in its most unrefined state. I can see them beyond their wounds. I can hear beyond their hurt, and I hold the faith and the light while they take that walk through the dark night of the soul. While many might fear this and feel it is cause for alarm, I know this is cause for celebration. This is the beginning of their rebirth and rising. It is a magical time.

It is my understanding that we grow through what we go through. Our trauma is our training, and reframing is our healing. To shift from being a victim of your past to the leader of your life looks like reframing your understanding of what has happened to you. Giving your pain purpose will ignite a passion you hadn't previously had access to. Respectfully, not everyone desires to become a leader directly in the area that they have experienced wounding, but so often, what we have experienced in life also influences what we choose to do with or lives. Frankly, some people do not desire to be a leader in the traditional meaning at all. When I discuss being the leader of your life, I am referring to achieving your own definition of success. It will require you healing and reframing your past to move past surviving and into thriving.

Turning our pain into purpose usually starts out as a direct response. People who have lost many loved ones become grief counselors. Victims of sexual abuse start foundations and movements to create awareness and end the cycle. Divorcees guide others going through break-ups. Doctors are frequently inspired by a traumatic event they witnessed or experienced in their youth. People become teachers when they realize the influence teachers have had on them, but it doesn't always end there.

People do not step into and stay in these roles without having a driving force pushing or pulling them in that direction. It is in our nature to take what happens to us and give it purpose. This is the power of reframing. You can stay a victim, marred with scars and wounds, or you can heal and serve. We may live out these dreams to right a wrong or correct something we perceive as broken. When we arrive at a resolution with our own wounding, our dreams, goals, and desires may naturally shift into something different.

Hurt people hurt people. Healed people heal people. It is that simple. If you stay stuck feeling sorry for yourself, you are choosing to stay stuck in separation and judgment. You are choosing the story of "why did this happen to me?" and "I am so alone in my suffering." The idea that no one could understand or relate to your pain is your ego. It is a false sense of being special in this way, that doesn't serve you or anyone else. This is an imperative part of taking responsibility for your impact.

Forcing people to deal with wounds that you refuse to tend to and heal within yourself, hurts them in response. You are sucking energy instead of transmuting your own pain. People will tire of being around you, which will solidify your belief that you are a burden and no one likes you. It is completely irresponsible, and I say this with the most powerful love I have to offer. I lay this out flat and clear because you have more to offer than that. However, no one can hold you to your potential if you are not willing to live up to it yourself. No one can force that upon you. You must choose it.

Once you choose it, you become available for guidance, and God will rush in with your personal support team. This may look like friends or family, but it can also be a complete stranger. We hear countless stories of the random person who showed up at the perfect time to deliver the most divine message. New mentors and guides will show up and you will have profound insights that seem to pop into your mind like whispers from the wind. Once you choose to open your heart to healing, the entire Universe will conspire in your favor.

If you choose to take responsibility for this knowledge, then it is time to do the work of healing and functioning as an empowered individual. If you are ready to do that work, starting with a therapist, trauma-appropriate support group, coach, or spiritual leader will help you facilitate the process. A professional's support is unmatched at this stage and will help you in obtaining clarity. I want to be very specific about my message here; we are not meant to do this work alone. We cannot see ourselves well enough to make the changes that we are meant to make. Trusting a professional to guide and reflect will accelerate your journey and can even make it fun.

If you did have a bullet wound, you wouldn't take the bullet out yourself and stitch your own wound. Stop trying to perform your own surgeries. The work of reframing often requires a second party support structure because you are causing a shift in perspective. While building this muscle, having a second person provides a new perspective, which can open up a whole world of possibility. Ultimately, reframing shifts the experience from an offense to an invitation.

To understand that a break-up isn't an end, but a new beginning, opens up a world of possibility. To comprehend that death is an invitation to live will have you choosing life more purposefully. To gather that abuse endured was an opportunity to expand your capacity for compassion is a gift for you to bring to this world.

For as long as we remain victims of our trauma, we keep the gift to ourselves. In this book, I will do and say everything I am guided to, to guide you back to love.

I will guide you home to your heart, where you have that wellspring of love that heals your wounded spirit. I will reframe, realign, and repurpose all things that cause separation so that you may walk yourself closer to the nucleus of the human spirit, where you will be able to identify that we are all one.

This is Impact. Accepting that you went through exactly what you went through so that you could guide others through it is understanding your role on the planet. It is your job to take on the work of transmuting pain into purpose so that your soul may reveal your passion. This is made possible with reframing. It is time you get serious about it if you are serious about being an alchemist, and if you are serious about being an alchemist, I have a tool for you that you can start applying today: NASR.

I teach this concept to every person in each of my programs because it is the most valuable and frequently used tool I have. NASR is an acronym for notice, acknowledge, stop, and redirect. This is a opportunity to shift your attitude and impact on a moment-to-moment basis. The more you use it, the better you get, so take opportunities to use it frequently.

'Notice' is the concept I have been pressing for the last two chapters. Notice everything. Become hyper-aware and observant. You can only shift what you can see, so it is time to take the veil down between you and your behaviors. Start to notice your projections, patterns, actions, reactions, language, judgments, and impact. Notice everything.

One of my colleagues jokes with me, "Damn you, Abby! All this awareness is trash! Now I have to be super responsible for myself!" We have a good laugh, but I know he means it. To choose to take account-ability for your impact is a responsibility. However, the good news is that it becomes second nature, and that is precisely the point. If you are committed to being your highest and best, you will make it to a pretty blissful state of living, in which having a positive impact is the only way to live. If you are doing this moment-to-mo-ment, that fog will lift and you will suddenly notice that you are thriving in life. So, notice all of it.

For the sake of sharing this tool, let's say you are shifting self-defensive patterns. You have to notice when you are offended, intimidated, off-put, checking out, getting annoyed, and of course, getting defensive.

Next, you must acknowledge what you notice. If you are really committed to this transformation, I one thousand percent recommend acknowledging out loud. Verbally articulating the acknowledgement step will accelerate the transmutation. This might sound like "I notice that I am offended, getting defensive, and check-ing out." You may decide to speak yourself all the way through it by saying something like, "I recognize that I am doing what I would normally do in this situation. I am pissed off and annoyed, and now mad that I am mad about this, and I don't want this cycle to continue."

Speaking these thoughts out loud facilitates process-ing. It also helps us disassociate with the thoughts and feelings when we responsibly let them out as words. This is valuable to do in front of a mirror or alone to get started. You are working to transmute your energy, not puke it up on someone for them to clean up. When we do this, we naturally hear ourselves in new ways. This alone opens up worlds we have never had available to us before.

Once you feel as though you have effectively noticed and acknowledged, it is time to stop. Stop the pattern, habit, or way of being right where it is. No more griping or sulking. To create muscle memory recognition, you can do something to the effect of clapping your hands or snapping your fingers to signal the stopping point.

There are some days when simply stopping feels impossible. At these times, it is important to remove yourself from the situation or conversation that is triggering your pattern. Remember, nothing is so important that you can't take at least a five minute (or five day) break and come back to it. Creating distance between you and the trigger will help you regroup and recalibrate so that you may choose the reaction and impact you truly want to have from choice, not impulse.

One other strategy when the trigger train is rolling full steam ahead is to actually choose how long you would like to stay triggered. For example, I have clients who come to a call complaining about an ongoing problem with a co-worker. When we use NASR, we notice what is actually being triggered and acknowledge it. This doesn't mean the emotional impact has subsided yet. In this case, I ask my client, "and how long would you like to stay mad for?"

I literally expect a timeframe answer. Usually, the first

time I do this with someone, they laugh at me and think I'm joking. When I ask again, they are already distracted from their emotion and start calculating how long they would like to stay in their emotion for. This response can range from five more minutes to five more days. I always grant them whatever timeframe they choose, but the point is that they are at choice.

From that point, I ask them to choose to have their emotion on purpose. "Take your seat as the mayor of Pity City," I joke with them, and even if they are still in their feelings, they get it and agree. Being at choice about our emotions changes the game. Instead, you are now *choosing* your own disempowered state of being, and let me tell you, that doesn't last long.

From here, we have the last step of redirection. I would like to start the last step by saying that this tool is ineffective if you skip a step. Skipping steps can be detrimental because you are rushing past understanding what is happening within you. Many folks want to go from noticing bad thoughts straight to redirecting their thoughts. Wrongo! I have taught this tool thousands of times and most people realize they use it naturally, but don't recognize it as a four-step process.

With this knowledge, identifying which step is missing or weak for you becomes much easier.

I encourage you to use NASR fully and in its defined order, and you will find yourself using it dozens of times per day. I also have an audio explanation of NASR on my Hearts Unleashed Podcast, episode #080 at heartsunleashed.com.

Redirecting is important, and it is not about positive affirmations. It's not about pretending to be okay when you are not. Redirection is all about you getting back into your own empowered energy. It's about you getting back to being you. So, when you consider redirection statements or activities, it is all about vibrating at your authentic frequency. That is why fluffy thoughts and affirmations that aren't true to your heart won't work.

Something that I do with my clients when discussing redirection is to create a toolbox for this step. I work with them to create a list of things to do depending on the time available for a reset. I will share my own.

If I have two to five minutes, I will have a dance party to one of my favorite anthem songs. If I have five to ten minutes, I will go outside, barefoot, breathe fresh air, and focus on nature and my body. With ten to twenty minutes, I will read my daily devotionals and journal. If I see it to be the most helpful, regardless of the quantity of time, I will pick up the phone and call my coach or a colleague to support a clearing process with me. Beyond thirty minutes, I may choose rollerblading, a surf session, writing, a bath, and more. The whole point is that I know what Abigail would love to do to feel like Abigail again. You must learn and utilize the resources available to get yourself back to being you.

By the time you have completed this exercise, you will feel empowered to break cycles, establish boundaries, identify and communicate needs, and more. This is my favorite and most effective tool of sustainable and lasting transformation. Use it regularly and you will experience your own magic of being able to alchemize judgment.

We have discussed many tools for you to take responsibility and accountability for yourself as an energetic being having a human experience. You have even more awareness and new resources to make powerful shifts from victim to leader. As a result of you living, you will make more memories. Life will happen, and the more you allow yourself to grow through what you go through, you will not be the same. You will not handle things the same. You will begin to elevate above these happenings when you are able to recognize that they are not about you.

An alchemist is a human aware of its true nature and power. An alchemist respects the Law of Impermanence, which is simply: nothing lasts. Everything passes, and when you respect that infinite truth, you will be liberated from the suffering of your humanness.

So, I challenge you to observe everything as temporary. View every situation and emotion as a breath in the wind. Let them come and go without watching any one of them too hard. I mean this for everything in life. When you understand that everything is temporary in nature, you can decide where you really wish to exert your energy. When you realize your own impermanence, you will take more responsibility for your time here.

This is the work of an alchemist; constantly expanding your consciousness beyond your being, to access the divinity in each situation. Find the holiness in every single interaction and choose your impact accordingly. You have been trimming that judgment tree. You are out on thinner limbs that require the use of different muscles, ones you've never used before. You are going further than you've ever gone, and it will take you further in life than you have ever been. Just keep climbing.

Chapter 7

Intolerance

Once you become aware of and take responsibility for your impact in the world, you will go through a phase in which you are highly sensitive to and intolerant of low vibrations and their subsequent manifestations. Similar to when people suddenly see the mess around them and start an Integrity Rampage, individuals in this phase will also have a heightened awareness of and reaction to people, places, and things that are out of alignment with their new value systems. As you begin to expect more of yourself, you naturally begin to see and expect more from others, as well. Ideas, feelings, and concepts that never seemed apparent before become glaringly obvious.

It can be as simple as the noises and mannerisms of others that you never noticed, to the fact that you can now tell when people are lying. Your shifts in awareness will cause shifts in tolerance. You may feel a natural resistance to this at first, but it is something you must also accept. Your preferences will change. A Friday night at a bar might not be so appealing any more. Men who treat women less than respectfully will become obvious and unattractive. People who gossip and complain will become exceptionally screechy to your ears. Being late on a payment is no longer acceptable. Saying yes to everything that everyone expects of you now feels empty and hollow.

Very specifically, the general language of others will be abrasive to your being; their shit talking, doubting, naysaying, ho-humming, paraphrasing, regurgitating, and more will all become cringeworthy because of everything you are unconditioning yourself from. I just want you to know how natural this is, and not to become discouraged or worried. This phase of the experience can sometimes be isolating. You may fear that you are losing touch with or growing apart from some individuals and that may be the case. What I want to give you hope about is the fact that this will lead to new conversations with new people in your new language. When you stay focused on the new, instead of the old, the transition becomes much smoother, and dare I say, even enjoyable.

Intolerance occurs because you have taken responsibility for your subconscious behaviors and you are hyperaware of your energy, and the energy of things around you. It is important to note: there is nothing wrong here! I repeat, there is nothing wrong. This is simply a transition phase, and I suggest you get pretty used to this feeling because it will occur for some time.

I will teach you how to transmute your newfound repulsion as to not simply slip into a new brand of judgment. I am not helping you raise your vibration as to consider yourself above or better than others, although it may feel like that at first. Once you pop your head up above water, away from the lower vibrations, you will naturally start to judge others, and even yourself, for having existed on that plane. Remember, there is nothing wrong, and it is just a phase.

This is a phase I like to call an Awareness Hangover. When your focus shifts and all of a sudden you can see all of the gunk gathering in the corners of your life, you will naturally question how you've never seen it all before. You will doubt your sense of discernment. You may feel some initial feelings of resentment that no one has pointed this out or taught you before but I want to teach you a valuable lesson right now: nobody is responsible for you.

That's right, my friend. It's crazy, I know, but nobody is responsible for saving you from yourself. That is your job. You can ask your Higher Power to help you, but no human can truly do the inner work for you that makes the change happen. That's all on you. The good news is in today's day and age you have endless resources to assist you in doing this work. I wrote this book to help you do exactly that, so before you get too bent out of shape and go on a blaming rampage, breathe. This is a relief. The lesson behind no one being responsible for you is: your life is yours. That's right, my friend, and what a relief. You can shift, change, transform, and follow your own inner authority all the way down the path of enlightenment.

You, like everyone else, may have people that you naturally take into account when making major life decisions, and that is a bit different. That is all fine, but you must ultimately remember that it is your sole (and soul) responsibility to live a great life. That will always be an inside job. We all awaken on our own time, so practice dropping judgment quickly and frequently if you feel late to the show or pissed that no one invited you sooner. It is all happening in divine time.

I will not dive too deeply into your role to lead others to a higher vibration, at least in this chapter. However, I will drop a breadcrumb about the fact that when you transcend lower order vibrations, you will shine brighter. Some people will react like a vampire to sunlight and others will gravitate like a bug to a lamp. Later in this book, I will teach you how to use your powers for the good of all, always. For now, let's keep focusing on you.

Everything you are suddenly noticing in your life that now doesn't match existed before your mental shift. These things weren't obvious because they all existed in harmony with a different vibration. They existed at the lower vibration that you were vibrating at. I remember my cousin once telling me a story about getting her son glasses at the age of four. She said she and her husband had no idea he was born with poor vision and she remembers crying tears of joy on the car ride home the day he got his glasses. My baby cousin was staring out of the window amazed by the brand-new way the world appeared to him. "Mom! The leaves on the trees! That's what trees look like?!" He proclaimed with newfound wonder. When you raise your vibe, you raise your clarity. Your vision suddenly shifts like putting on a brand new pair of glasses and you can see a whole new world. This is a subconscious shift, and the projection of your mind brings a new reality into focus. As a result, you also naturally raise your standard for living. You are able to see options and choose a higher standard of living.

When this first occurs, you will find yourself exceptionally sensitive to all of these awarenesses. People you have known your whole life will, both literally and figuratively, look different. Your workplace can become more or less inspiring. Family and friend gatherings will feel different. Similar to too much light burning when the doctor dilates your eyes, when you dilate your mind and heart, too much negativity can feel abrasive. You can also start to feel confused, disappointed, and out of place. This is an example of vulnerability. You are essentially raw to this new way of being and thinking. I want to remind you, there is nothing wrong here.

Kind of like a brand new baby, it cannot protect, feed, or care for itself. You want to nurture the new baby and surround it with good energy and plenty of love. When you suddenly recognize that you have been being an ungrateful ass most of your life and decide to give that all up, you are essentially being born again. You are choosing a new life. Therefore, you are in your infancy of integrity.

If you have recognized that you have been in protective mode your entire life and finally decide to put your fists down, you will feel incredibly vulnerable. To choose to stop fighting and walk with your hands by your sides, all you will be able to think about for the first while is that your neck, chest, and stomach are exposed. It may have you on high alert for a while, and that is okay, too. There is nothing wrong. You are simply learning a new way of thinking and being…and in this case, trusting.

Think about it, you have years, likely decades of old patterns, and when you uncover certain things in transformation, it is often in a 'once and for all' kind of way. There will be so many things that you cannot unsee or unhear. Your newfound commitment to integrity will make your self-sabotaging choices too obvious to tolerate from yourself and others. Once you realize that you date unavailable men to avoid the sting of rejection, there really is no going back. Once you understand that you eat to avoid feeling, that pastry looks like a pile of bugs. Once you value your body and life, a cigarette can be seen for the cancer stick that it is. When you realize that you use sex to feel loved, it will lose its flare. Again, nothing wrong here.

It may seem like I am out to ruin all of your fun, but I am here to provide you hope as well. When you raise your vibration, you will simply subscribe to a different brand of fun. It will be a more wholesome and fulfilling flavor of fun and will have a more positive impact. Double wins. I will bring hope to the plate about your newfound fun in later chapters. For now, let's figure out what you can do about this new intolerance for low vibe shit.

Remember to give yourself some grace. This transition will take time and practice, and I am going to teach you a few tools to empower the shift. Even if you know better and don't act better, you will *know* you are choosing not to do better. This will naturally be out of integrity and you will become intolerant of being out of integrity over time.

Let's start with one of my favorite parts of integrity. Setting up and maintaining boundaries, standards, expectations, and conditions of satisfaction. Yippee! I am seriously excited to teach you all about these because it is such a good opportunity for you to take your power and life back, and I love nothing more than seeing you do that. We are getting to the good stuff, people!

When we are operating at a low frequency, the barrier to entry in our life is low as well. We let people walk all over us, mistreat and disrespect us, and their energy can impact us greatly. Surprisingly, when we operate at this level, we *think* we have boundaries, but they are really barriers. This is an example of energetically walking through life with your fists up, ready to fight any mf-er that crosses you. You know these people in the world. You might even be one of them; one of those, "I freakin' dare you sons of bitches" kind of fighters in life, just lookin' for a fight. This is a survival mechanism of misdirected aggression from unhealed mommy, daddy, and sibling wounds. Don't be one of those people in the world. Go back through these last few chapters and heal your stuff.

The boundaries I am referring to now are the ones that establish *for others* what you will and won't tolerate in your life. This is where you stop giving your power and authority away. Another great book that I recommend for this transition phase is "The Four Agreements" by Don Miguel Ruiz. It will help you understand more about impeccable integrity and four agreements to live by that will empower your decision to live in alignment with your highest good.

You teach people how to treat you. When you wake up to integrity and higher vibrations, you must also establish new standards and expectations for yourself, others, and life itself. This takes practice, so don't lose hope just because you start seeing yourself different and others start questioning why you don't want a third beer. When you know you don't want to do old things and be the old you, you must first grant yourself permission to change before others can see and accept the new you.

I remember this vividly after I began my sobriety journey. Going back home was a challenge for me because I was quite the life of the party in my younger years. During transformation, I actually recognized this part of me as a jester and didn't want to do the song and dance anymore. I felt some peer pressure sometimes, but I knew that the pressure to perform was nowhere near the Integrity Hangover of knowing better and not doing better. When I would compromise, I always regretted it. After a few times of not honoring my word to myself, I knew I was going to stop negotiating my own standards for life.

Speaking of standards, it's time to set some. All of the lessons in this chapter are an invitation to start taking inventory of your life.

- What no longer suits me?
- What have I outgrown?
- What am I outgrowing?
- Who am I without all those old habits, patterns, and ways of being?
- What do I want?
- How do I want life to go?
- What are *my* preferences?
- What are my priorities?
- What is important to me?
- Who do I really want to be in this world?
- What is my definition of success?
- What would I want someone to say about me at my funeral?
- What would I *fear* they would have to say!?
- What legacy do I want to leave?

I could keep this list of questions going on for days in the realm of integrity because this is where you are establishing your new standard of living. In fact, I work with my clients on exactly this work in my Time to Shine program available on abigailgazda.com.

I encourage you to get yourself a notebook and put these questions on the first page, and once a month or once a quarter come back to them. Life is never a once-and-for-all-made-it-to-the-point-I-can-finally-relax kind of deal. If you are committed to being an alchemist, you will constantly shapeshift into the next, evolved version of yourself. You will often hear me refer to being your 'highest and best' and I want you to remember this isn't a destination. If you are always allowing yourself to evolve, you are always your highest and best because you are always a collection of everything you have learned, and you are also applying it intentionally. This is always the best you can do and you will always do better when you know better.

Plants grow from the inside out, and so do humans. Keep allowing yourself to bud and blossom as you discover new parts of yourself along the way and as you do, you will require new conditions of satisfaction, or COS. COS looks like the standards and expectations you have for life. If you are operating from old wounds, a common expectation is 'bad things happen to good people.' This is a really disempowering belief to project because you will manifest it everywhere.

When you heal old wounds, you can start allowing your beliefs to fuel a great life. This is when people start resonating with mantras such as 'it feels good to feel good and I deserve to feel good.' When you allow yourself to believe that life and people are good, you are not constantly protecting yourself from threats and disappointment.

Having COS is like putting an order in with God. It can be seen as a form of prayer in a sense. Now, this can be a bit tricky because people confuse prayers to God with letters to Santa. They are not the same. Establishing conditions of satisfaction for your life looks more like asking for health, wealth, and guidance. This is specific to you living at your highest and best for the good of all, not the good of your ego. That is why when I ask my clients who they are and what they want, we have to filter through what they don't want and what they think they want based on their life experience.

Prayers, requests, boundaries, standards, expectations, and conditions of satisfaction are all in alignment with your commitment to being the leader that you are in this world. This is about you becoming intolerant of anything less than your best and a willingness to release anything that no longer serves you. This will take earthly and divine support if you are deeply committed to winning the game of life and if you have made it this far into this book, I have a whole lot of faith that you are.

Setting yourself up for a new life can feel daunting, and I want you to know that it can be. I will not sell it like an infomercial. It will not always be easy to tell someone "no" or to have a tough conversation. It will give you the sweats to establish boundaries with people and you will get pushback. It can be gag-worthy to tell a friend they are bringing you down with their negativity. And I want to tell you it's okay. There is nothing wrong here. This is growth and it is natural. It won't always be easy, but it will always be worth it.

I highly recommend journaling during your transformation and for a guide on how to journal effectively, check out my Hearts Unleashed Podcast episode # 078. This will help you understand some key steps to moving through your thoughts and making choices that you are proud of. Staying committed to that will create a life you are satisfied with and fulfilled by.

Your life is yours, my dear. You choose how it goes. You choose what you engage in. You choose who you interact with and you choose your impact. Get clear on the life you want to lead so you can get in integrity with it, and you will be living a life you absolutely love.

Chapter 8

Completion

I have thoroughly explained integrity as a pillar of life so far in this book. I have intentionally gone into the depths on topics and baselined them in ways that you will be able to see yourself more clearly. This is to support you as an alchemist bringing everything back into the love energy, and there will be more on that in the upcoming Pillar. This Pillar has been put together to offer you awareness around your automatic, or default, ways of being.

No more inauthenticity. No more impulsive impact and reactivity. No more victimhood. No more acting out of integrity about what you know. You must own your responsibility for this life, and when you do, you can step into your unique role in moving humanity forward.

This next theory that I am going to teach about is the concept of completion. When it comes to integrity, completion is by far the most important component to facilitate the work and create a forward momentum. One of my favorite things to say about completion is that you cannot run a marathon with a ball and chain on your foot. Completion is the concept of healing your wounds to the point that they no longer hold negative energy or keep you operating at a low frequency. Unhealed wounds disempower you and hold you back.

You will know you are successfully practicing completion when you are consistently less triggered in your life on a day-to-day or even moment-by-moment basis. Transformation itself is about being able to live empowered for long durations of time and to recover from disempowerment quickly and frequently. I share this because I believe that many people confuse being transformed or enlightened as being perfectly peaceful, blissful, and tolerant. It is hardly that. Much like you cannot exclude judgment from your humanness, you cannot rid your life of unexpected hardship, disappointments, and triggers.

Our transformation is a reflection of our capacity to be with any and everything from a clear place of nothingness. Nothingness representing a lack of association or definition; said one other way, complete detachment. It is to have no need to engage with our humanness or ego when we encounter something that would be considered upsetting or troubling. This also goes in the opposite direction, and the entire spectrum in between. You can also be detached from good or great things that cause ego-based reactions. This is a mastery level of 'coming from nothing.' When we hold no reference for how things *should* be, we are open to all the ways things *can* be.

This is made possible by the constant clearing and releasing available through completion. It is to empty every bag you carry your emotional weight in. It is to release your needs as a means for validation and gratification. This work is the work of someone committed to living clearly and liberated, and to exist as freely as this realm can offer.

The act of completion is saying what there is to say and doing what there is to do to put a period at the end of a sentence in your life.

- It looks like closing a chapter in the book of your life.
- It's tying up loose ends.
- It's healing an open wound.
- It's removing a thorn.
- It's delivering unspoken communications.
- It's reconciling debts.
- It's handling unkept promises.
- It's ending toxic behaviors and relationships.
- It is feeling unfelt feelings.
- It is fully grieving loss and disappointment.
- It is digesting untended thoughts, feelings, and emotions.

Take a good look at that list. Sometimes, we too quickly scan things that are in a listed format, and I want you to examine each bullet point on a deeply personal level. Each of these components are energetic blocks, stagnant in your body. I like to refer to them as gunk.

This will be helpful as we proceed through the Alignment Pillar. Consider yourself as a vessel for love to flow to and through; if you are clogged, flow is restricted. I will be teaching you how to clear the gunk and become a true alchemist, one who can come from that space of nothingness.

I will be rigorously specific about getting all the gunk out as we go on. I want you to imagine getting to the point that you are no longer digging or scraping but wiping and polishing: *that* clean, *that* clear, *that* committed to being a true alchemist. So, I invite you to read over that list again and locate where each one exists in your body. What are you doing to rid loose ends, debts, and disappointments? What unkept promises, grief, and unspoken words haunt you? If you allow yourself to consider each one seriously, you can find them in your memory banks and you store them like excess fat in your body. Until you acknowledge and work them out, they will stay stored in your energetic body and weigh you down.

That constant sore neck? Your back pain and migraines? The arthritis, tendonitis, and countless other symptoms are the storage of low frequency gunk stuck to the walls of you. If you considered doing any and all of the things on this list, just take a deep breath and imagine how much resolution you would experience in your life. People often think success is about what there is to do ahead of them. You already know what to do to succeed and exactly how to do it all. It is the gunk that *stops* you from doing it. Success is made available when you clean up the messes you have all over your life, past and present.

Completion is commonly mistaken for 'closure.' However, I would invite you to understand that closure is from your ego. The illusion of closure is believing that getting answers from people you feel owe you an explanation will bring you peace. It looks like trying to figure out and understand circumstances prematurely just so you can feel better or have momentary relief.

Closure is forceful. Closure is surface level and contingent upon external factors. We sense we need closure when we can't seem to make sense of things or when outcomes seem unfair to us. We operate from a space of manipulation when seeking 'closure' because it is not closure we are seeking. It is a false sense of control we desire.

Completion, on the other hand, is about transmuting the previously painful energy or circumstance into something that empowers us. It is properly digesting an experience and its energy, to bring you back to love and gratitude. Closure is a band-aid fix for an issue that needs heart surgery. Completion is a whole new diet that will help you obtain and maintain heart health; literally and figuratively.

I have mentioned turning your pain into your purpose. Taking the time to create completion around unhealed wounds, broken relationships, and traumatizing experiences will cut cords that keep us held back from going forward in life. You cannot go forward with a ball and chain on your foot. You cannot soar with emotional baggage weighing you down.

Again, completion is about saying what there is to say and doing what there is to do, in order to feel truly complete with a situation. This can allow you to energetically remove it from your body.

When we refuse to process something, it stays stagnant within us. When we allow ourselves to examine it fully, we can gain a better understanding of the pain it caused, the conclusions we drew, and the survival mechanisms we created to defend ourselves against what we perceived as threats. When we are incomplete with our past, we project that pain into our future, recreating it time and time again.

I love to remind people that the universe will continue to teach you a lesson until you learn it. If you refuse to reach completion with events that have occurred in your life, you will run into parallel circumstances and individuals, both showing up to teach you that lesson over, and over again. It is your responsibility to take heed.

You must slow down enough to recognize the subconscious manifestations trying to communicate a need within your body. In my work, it is common knowledge that our childhood wounds are what shape so much of our personalities, patterns, and preferences. Who we are is based on the occurrences of our formative years. It is a sliding scale of ending up nothing like our parents or exactly like our parents and so many of our decisions are meant to match or defy our upbringing. This isn't always life threatening but it does limit our ability to understand ourselves and our authentic expression.

I want to remind you; the Universe will teach you this lesson until you learn it - you came here to be an authentic expression of love.

You did not come here only to be an extension of your parents, nor is it your natural expression to be the opposite of your parents. Your biggest job here is to know, own, love, and share yourself. You must discover your own preferences and definitions of success, meaning, and purpose. Throughout life, everyone and everything will come and go. You must recognize that *you* are your only constant in life. Therefore, your greatest task is to master yourself and live fully unleashed.

We aren't exactly taught or encouraged to do this in school, and unless we had highly self-aware and conscious parents, we were probably raised in a traditional household in which emotional intelligence wasn't a dinner table topic. This isn't bad or wrong, it just has its own set of consequences. One of those consequences is that our upbringing had an impact on our self-image. We don't have to grow up in a broken home or have had to live through painful trauma to draw certain disempowering conclusions about ourselves.

Even with well-intentioned parents and a generally healthy household, events occur during childhood that can cause us to draw conclusions about ourselves, others, a Higher Power, and the world. Involuntarily, our brain develops and archives on certain days more than others, leaving imprints upon our body and mind. Some of these specific memories produce feelings of unlovability, inadequacy, or unworthiness. These imprints aren't always drastic or obvious, but if they go unidentified and unhealed, we can struggle with the subtle manifestations attempting to reveal our subconscious beliefs.

If we do not heal childhood wounds, we may find ourselves stuck in a looping pattern of manifesting evidence of our perceived flaws. Let's be clear, these wounds are a function of being human. There is nothing anyone did to cause them. They are no one's fault and there is nothing wrong with you. There is no good or bad about them, they are just a part of the human condition.

What is so important to understand is that while we cannot prevent them, we must heal them, or they will keep popping up in your life as general annoyances. They will show up in your career, relationships, finances, and more. You may constantly get overlooked for the promotion, never make it past the second date, have repetitive toxic relationships, consistently struggle with your relationship with food or substances, or always find a new bill in your mailbox. There tends to be this perpetual challenge that gets the unhealed, incomplete person down. Many people who struggle with these disempowering beliefs often wonder why they have been dealt such a tough hand in life. It is because the childhood wounds have gone unidentified.

Beyond that, you will find blame instead of a true root cause that exists within you. Blame, resentment, and rejection are all forms of judgment that will distract you from ever arriving to completion. Thus, you will also feel like you are missing a major key to a full life. You will feel incomplete and unfulfilled as a result of this deeply seated belief, and your unwillingness to examine it. You must acknowledge and complete this pain in order to truly shift and see new results in your life and relationships.

Besides repetitive manifestations, incompletion also looks like forever recurring conversations in your head. Unspoken words. Arguments had. Experiences you've witnessed that took your power or innocence away from you in such a way that you still feel powerless. Pain inflicted. Dominance asserted without permission.

I am here to help you understand why you have repetitive, intrusive thoughts that never seem to go away. The answer is incompletion.

I am going to provide you with some tools for completion work and I want to start with an important preface: completion work is something that I highly suggest doing with a professional. As mentioned previously, we cannot see ourselves fully, nor can we see our trauma fully. In order to digest it properly and transmute it effectively, having the support of a professional will move you through spaces that you are otherwise afraid to go through. If you could do it on your own, you would.

One thing I do not suggest is expecting to do completion work with a friend. I, myself, go to a professional for this work. When we go to friends and family for this true work, they cannot hold the space of nothingness to appropriately process our thoughts, feelings, and experiences. It is challenging for someone untrained to listen and add nothing so that you can explore your own energy. Others' inclusion in your completion can cloud your experience of working your way entirely through it. This is why I suggest someone who can hold space for you, and even draw out every bit of the incompleteness.

If you are weeding a garden and pull too hard, you will likely break the root, leaving some of it to remain in the dirt and grow back. Completion is slow and thorough, aiming to get it all out. Sometimes, you leave something behind and have to weed again, but once you finally get the root, your body will tell you. You will have a deep sense of knowing you are complete.

This work takes time, intention, commitment, willingness, and vulnerability. Be kind with yourself. Focus on your grace. In my personal and professional opinion, completion is the most important work there is to do in all of life, because it makes everything else possible. To do it will afford you the opportunity to cut the chains of your pain and past so that you can move forward into your future joyously.

Once you learn the concept and feel empowered, another way to work through creating completion in your life is to communicate with people that you know you are incomplete with. The key word here is empowered. If you are disempowered, then it is your ego seeking closure, not your soul creating completion. You can imagine how thin the line between these two are and you must know the difference before using my next suggestion.

This can be scary and may require some support and accountability. This is primarily why I encourage you to seek a professional for guidance. However, if you feel confident about this, make a list of people you know you are incomplete with. I like inviting my clients to do this energetically. They get out a notebook and make the longest list they can of people they know they are incomplete with. This can go as far back as childhood, and all the way through your life to the present. It doesn't matter what level of incomplete you are at with someone to put them on that list. The Universe will start conspiring in your favor. You may see them on the street. You may get a random phone call or text from them. You may 'all of a sudden' get a friend request on social media. They may show up to you in a dream or meditation. This is the universe affording you the opportunity to create completion in your life.

Next, I am going to teach you how to have powerful conversations to develop your completion. You can apply this lesson to your energetic completion list and your interactions from this day forward. However you decide to use it, this is your access to not only releasing old gunk, but to prevent collecting any new gunk as well.

A conversation to completion is a pretty simple concept: you do not leave the conversation until both people feel that they have said everything they need to say in order to feel complete.

When I started to do this in my life...which I promise took some learning...it always proved to be worth the discomfort of learning a new skill. When I learned to practice conversations to completion in my life, I had less new baggage each and every day. I was simultaneously completing bigger traumas from my past. I started to feel lighter and more liberated to express my more authentic self.

When I wasn't struggling with traumas of my past, my authentic self started to reveal herself, naturally. My thoughts became more focused on creative endeavors, trips I wanted to plan, places I wanted to see, and things I wanted to do. When I began to free myself from the clutches of my past, my life simply became more fun. The more fun you have, the more fun you *can* have, because it feels good to feel good. It is the Cycle of Love I referred to, in action.

Completing your past will make things available to you that you could have never imagined. You think you have big dreams now. When you release yourself from the prison of your past, you will attain your greatest goals and have to consider new ones because you will be able to climb even higher without the emotional baggage. That being said, let's talk about having conversations to completion.

I'm going to teach you a few key methods of communication that will empower a conversation to completion. Whether it is a disagreement, a tough truth to share, or closing a chapter of the past, when it comes to having a conversation, it can bring up natural nerves and anxiety. What this also tends to do is bring up our own insecurities. This will have us listening and speaking through the filters of our past, so, instead I am going to teach you a few fundamental steps you can follow to best communicate, without getting your own perception and projections in the way.

If you are committed to creating completion with someone, it is helpful to share these cues with your partner in order to empower *both* of you in a conversation to completion:

Some steps and cues you can use are:

- "I have something vulnerable I need to share…"
- If it helps, share the emotions first (i.e. "I am nervous, uneasy, concerned…").
- Then, share as authentically as tolerable. Really stretch here.
- Listener: create space for someone's share by not interrupting.
- An empowering response to a vulnerable share can look like:
- "What I heard you say was…" to reflect what the listener thinks they heard the person sharing say.
- This will allow the listener to reflect the share to acknowledge comprehension.
- Allow for the person sharing to confirm or correct the listener's reflection to ensure they feel heard, seen, and fully understood.
- Reflect and correct until both people feel clear and on the same page.
- A follow-up to a share can be something to the effect of "The way I received that was…" or "What I made that mean is…"

- Again, allow space for the response without interrupting.
- Reflect and correct again, until both feel clear and understood.
- To begin ensuring full communication and completion, one may ask, "Does that feel complete for you?" or "Is there you anything else you need to say to be complete?"
- Allow for more to come up and say what does openly. Another incompletion may be identified and sorted out, as well. These are very thorough questions, and when they are asked multiple times, we genuinely search our heart for the, "Yes, that is complete."
- Do this back and forth until both parties can say for themselves, "I feel complete."

Prioritizing this exercise can help people experience clarity while also allowing room for the other person's experience and emotions. This conversation is not one meant for virtue signaling, moralizing, criticizing, or judging. The quickest way to alchemize judgment is through understanding. To enter into a conversation to completion implies a commitment to understanding the other person/situation, not *just* to get their point or pain across. It is a conversation to create space for allowing others to express themselves, be heard, and seen.

Conversations to completion occur when both people are committed to being one hundred percent authentic in their communication. This approach almost always ends up in some form of mutual understanding.

Simply because you both maintain a different perspective doesn't mean you don't walk away without at least understanding, and likely, respecting each other.

Now, you may be rolling your eyes thinking, "Good Lord, Abigail! Are we really supposed to do that all day, every day?!?" The answer is yes, and as I have shared throughout this book, the more you do it the better you get at it, and the less it seems like work in the first place. When I started doing this in my life, people were taken by surprise, and yet, they leaned right into the conversation and questions. This amount of powerful questioning and communication is a relief in the world. We spent the last few chapters talking about your impact, and if you are committed to having conversations to completion, your impact will be unique, transformative, and lasting.

I encourage you to have every single conversation lead to completion. Never feel strange for making sure someone feels complete with their interaction with you. If you do this, you will lay your head on your pillow at night feeling like you've checked every box there is to check. You will rest peacefully. You will start each new day anew. You will stop adding baggage to your life, allowing you to be freed up for all of your passions and your purpose. This occurs because you have chosen to restore and maintain your integrity in all aspects of your life.

In order to get better at this, I would like to teach you an awareness tactic I like to call See Something, Say Something. I pinky promise you, I was not perfect at completion conversations when I first started them. In fact, I was a little nervous and insecure about making sure someone was complete before they walked away. What was even more detrimental, I would be afraid to admit that I was not complete with a conversation before they walked away.

Someone might have said something that didn't make sense to me and for days, I would dwell on it, feeling insecure about what they meant by what they said. Once I committed to having conversations to completion, if I didn't have the courage to complete the conversation right in the moment, I made a new promise to complete it sometime in the near future.

"Hey Johnny, you said something the other day that really stuck with me. You made a remark that 'I do that thing when I talk' and I didn't quite understand what you meant by it. It has sort of been bothering me and I just wanted to communicate that and contact you to get some clarity. Do you mind explaining what you meant by that statement?" You can then use the cues I gave you to have a full completion conversation, leaving both of you walking away from the call feeling empowered, heard, seen, understood, and accepted.

Cool, added benefit: people secretly love when you come back for completion because it gives them freedom, too. Whether the incompletion is communicated or not, your withholding your truth acts like a thread between the two of you, energetically tying each other together. To cut those cords sets them free in ways they didn't know they were being tied down. People love believing they have no qualms with others. Clearing and completing is a contribution to humanity as a whole. It is a generous civic duty.

For me, calling people back was transformational, but after a while, I got tired of having to pick up the phone to let people know I was incomplete with them. I didn't want to do that anymore, so I started taking responsibility mid-conversation. If something triggered me or if something seemed off, I would call it out immediately. I would say what I needed to say and I would make sure that I listened to them as well.

I got really good at doing this in the moment. So good, that I stopped sweating when I knew I needed to do it! Now, it is a natural part of my conversation and people love it. They appreciate it and even expect it. Oftentimes, I will be complimented on how thorough I am in a conversation and how it makes a difference in people feeling complete. People notice it. People will notice you. You will leave people feeling better than when they came to you. You will leave hearts more unleashed then when you met them. Get this: you will even be teaching them how to carry this skill into their own life through your modeling and integrity. Ripple effect, baby! *This* is having a true and lasting positive impact and that is what you are here for. When you master it, you can provide that for yourself and for others.

If you do this throughout your life, you will be living with integrity. Your conversations, projects, agreements, and promises will feel solid and complete. Not in a 'once and for all' kind of way, but in a functional and sustainable way. You will consistently feel empowered, enlivened, and fulfilled by your lack of attachments and incompletions. This is the employed part of integrity; doing what you know to do, when you know to do it, the way you know it is meant to be done. This is *being* a person of your word.

Always remember, your word creates your world. The quality and direction of your life is one hundred percent reliant upon the quality of your relationships. This directly includes the quality of your conversations. If you take the quality of your conversations seriously and bring them all to completion, you will certainly be thriving in life. You will be alchemizing all conversations back to love and this will have the greatest impact on your ability to naturally be in integrity *everywhere* else; health, wealth, spirituality, and more. As an active alchemist, you will feel integrous, confident, liberated, and in love with the life that you are deliberately creating.

Chapter 9

Integration

As we begin to wrap up the Integrity Pillar, I would like to name the tool that I have been indirectly teaching you throughout this pillar; integration. True integration is about the alchemy of healing. When it comes to the healing work, integrating your shadow side and trauma is to include it in your identity instead of suppress or deny it. This means that it is actually possible for you to reach a level of acceptance that frees you of suffering from past wounds. This doesn't eliminate the memory, it alchemizes the energy charge of the memory from triggering and disempowering, to not having a charge at all. I want to share the absolute blessing that integration work is and what it can make available for yourself and your life.

When we take an honest look inward and locate the parts of us we have not seen or accepted, we are given a new choice. Integration is choosing to include every facet of ourselves in our life; full self-acceptance. This is a whole and complete expression of yourself as an energetic being having a human experience.

If you think about all the versions of you, you can only go as far as the one you leave behind. If there is a part of you that you refuse to accept, then you have separated yourself into different identities and that rejected part will hold you back. You cannot experience full liberation unless you liberate the full you.

Throughout this book, we have created a lot of awareness about the many facets of your being. Another aspect of integration is applying all of your new awareness directly to your life. This is a true shift from knowledge to wisdom and knowing to owning. This means embedding the truths you have discovered into the depths of your being to reach peace, not just going through the motions because you are chasing a desired, external result. Performative Spirituality is about as satisfying as having a classic car with no engine. Sure, it looks great in the driveway, but the rubber never hits the road. Eventually, it's just another thing to polish without getting to enjoy the fruits of your labor.

A great example of this is when people decide to become spiritual and buy books on gemstones and essential oils. They start doing what they believe meditation and journaling is. They start listening to motivational speakers, but the words are lost on them. They start attending retreats, seminars, workshops and go into debt doing so. Then, they start walking, talking, dressing, and acting like the other folks who they see there.

Listen friend, I am all about 'acting as if' you already have the life you want, but if you do not take this Integrity Pillar seriously, you will find yourself feeling further away from your desires than when you started, because you will also be struggling with imposter syndrome. You cannot add abundance on top of scarcity. You must remove scarcity to make room for abundance. You must learn to transmute scarcity into grief. Then, you process grief into belief and from belief, you have access to possibility. Abundance lives in possibility. If you are not willing to bridge that gap one plank at a time, you will find yourself spiraling in self-doubt of your newfound 'spirituality.'

The bridge is the stages of transformation; Self Discovery, Self Development, Self Mastery, and Transcendence. You must do the inner work of transformation to have the skills of alchemizing any and all judgment. This is *actually* less work than Performative Spirituality. Many people want to gloss over their b.s. and pretend they're fine, but I will tell you a secret that you probably didn't know that you already know: pretending is utterly exhausting. Pretending to be happy, healthy, wealthy, abundant, put together, satisfied, and in love is some of the hardest work you could be doing. All of this pretending to avoid admitting you are struggling is slowly stealing all of your power.

Attempting to acquire abundance to negate a scarcity mindset is as effective as putting icing on a mud pie. No bueno, compadre. You must clear your head and heart space and the Universe will happily take care of the rest and provide countless blessings. I will teach you how to receive them in the upcoming chapter; Alignment Pillar.

Since we spent the last chapter discussing completion, I would like to start the integration lesson with forgiveness. This can get messy, because we think we can just 'get over it' or forgive and forget but I am sure you already know that is not necessarily the case. We can't really grasp why we have completed something or written someone off and cut them out of our life and yet, still manifest people and circumstances that pour salt in the same wound.

Trigger warning: I have specifically chosen to use the most widely relatable trigger that people are chained to for life if they cannot learn effective completion, forgiveness, and integration; rape, molestation, and/or sexual abuse of any sort. I have worked with and supported hundreds of people through the process of healing this wound and becoming thriving individuals. This is a wound that can leave a lifelong scar that affects countless relationships, experiences, opportunities, and overall well-being of a person. Sexual trauma is rampant in humanity and you are always one degree away from a case, if you are not that case. I invite you to open up your heart and mind to that fact and practice sensitivity about those around you who may be affected by this experience.

If you are reading this and feeling that retrigger, breathe. I am going to hand you a key to your freedom right now so just read slowly and take small breathing breaks if it supports you. I have already said it in this book. Every action is a holy interaction. This can be an offensive statement in this context, I know. Just keep reading. There are no mistakes in this Universe. The source of every single thing in existence is Love.

Does it always make sense to us? Absolutely not. Does it seem right or fair? Hell no. Does it seem grotesque and inhumane? Most definitely *and* there are no mistakes. There is a divine order to everything happening. The truth about these situations is that they can be so painful in the moment and on such a personal level that we cannot expand our consciousness beyond the pain to see a bigger picture. We cannot imagine how or why this plays out on a much larger scale and honestly, many never do find out why because they never take on authentic healing, forgiveness, and integration. They stay stuck in grief because they never transmute the judgment.

If you are reading and have directly been assaulted, it is important to state that you have every right to have every thought, feeling, and reaction you have to your experience; even to what you are reading right now. Stay in it. Feel everything fully, because it is through processing that you will be granted your freedom. You are the only person on this entire planet that can set yourself free from your struggle. Your trauma is not your fault, and it is your responsibility to heal it. You get to create your internal state of peace, gratitude, bliss, and joy.

Completion is about compassion, and I am inviting you to find compassion for your trauma and those who played a role in it. I mentioned that many never reach completion because they never process and transmute the judgment. It can be incredibly painful. There may be a lot of blame and judgment for the situation and those involved. This can include resentment of the predator or a friend or family member we felt neglected or betrayed by. We can blame ourselves or the circumstances. We may find fault in a situation we put ourselves in that compromised our safety, discernment, or decision-making abilities, and hold ourselves and others in contempt for all the pain we have experienced since.

This can cause layers of pain and suffering that goes on for years or decades. To take on releasing this pain, completion will look like exploring it. When I work with clients, I carefully work with them on recalling the experience, reminding them that they are currently safe in our conversation and that there is no threat at the moment. I make it safe to navigate the memory and we take a deep look at the pain it caused. We spend time observing the wound like two doctors hovering over a patient on an operating table. We identify the root cause and we tend to it. We treat the wound. In this example, we examine the trust issues, the innocence taken, the terror, the shame and guilt, the helplessness, and the feeling of the irreversible damage done. Many more thoughts, feelings, and body sensations come up as we do the work and we move through the process together. We don't rush through this procedure. We carefully discuss each aspect of the wound and take on the healing work.

To revisit this experience can be terrifying, upsetting, disruptive, and more. Essentially, that is the goal. The objective is to disrupt this memory as to remove it. Without ever tending to this wound effectively, it exists lodged in the energetic body and has physical, mental, and emotional symptoms. It can be a sensitive wound, like operating on the spine, but we proceed nonetheless. The reason anyone agrees to this process is because living with the symptoms has become more painful than dealing with it. If the operation means liberation, the client will take on this work no matter how uncomfortable it may seem. I have witnessed this liberation occur right before my very eyes. It is the most remarkable transformation to witness a beautiful human heal the pain of this trauma.

Completion, healing, and integration is not complete until you are able to arrive at an understanding that this occurrence was *for* you. Again, that never makes it right or fair by any means. This is not a way to justify this experience, it is a means of empowering you past your pain. The pain is not where you were meant to stop or stay. Pain of any kind is meant to take us somewhere, teach us something, and prepare us for the most unimaginable task of our unique leadership. If you have experienced this type of trauma, you have a unique healing process to go through, and this is important because where we are in the evolution of humanity, there will be more of this to occur.

I would never wish such pain on anyone, and from what I can see in today's world is that we are awakening to exactly how prevalent such crimes against humanity are. If people stayed quiet and suffered in silence, we would never be able to make a dent in healing this Collective wound, and we are. We are doing our best to raise the Collective frequency to more collaboration, community, and connection. It will take those who have suffered trauma to alchemize their pain into purpose and take charge to shift the paradigm of this plague.

I invite you to consider that you agreed to this life before you came here. Imagine that just before selecting the particular life circumstance to teach you the soul lessons of this round on earth, you saw the agenda items for your life and the cost of entry was agreeing to what was on that list. You chose the day, time, location, gender (even if you have shifted that in this plane), orientations, family, lessons, and more. You agreed to it all because you are an energetic being having a human experience. This skin bag of bones is a vehicle for your soul to play in this dimension. I do not say that to disrespect the body, but to provide you with some perspective that anything can happen to this body, and it will not affect your soul if you transcend the human experience. You can suffer trauma, lose limbs, organs can malfunction, be disfigured, etc, and you can still live a full life. We even see many examples of this from birth. People who are born with a disability, illness, or deformation often live fuller lives than able-bodied people and I find that particularly fascinating.

I will never forget growing up with my cousin, Luke, who was born with epidermolysis bullosa. It is a rare skin condition that causes fragile, blistering skin due to even minor rubbing, touch, or injury. It affected him internally and externally resulting in esophageal deterioration and multiple surgeries. Luke was born this way. Doctors told his parents he wouldn't live past three months, then, three years. His mom, a nurse, left her work and became Luke's full-time nurse. He required an extensive daily routine of cleansing wounds and changing bandages and this young man had every reason to not live a full life or enjoy the one he was given.

Believe me when I say, Luke-O, as we called him in the family, was the most grateful human being I have ever known. Sure, he had days that he didn't feel well but I specifically remember how his commentary about how cool the sky looked and how stoked he was to get to the ocean in his balloon tire wheel-chair gifted to him by the Make-A-Wish Foundation. Luke became one of the ambassador children for epidermolysis bullosa, met celebrities, and raised millions of dollars to find a cure. He was also an early advocate and promoter of holistic remedies for EB and even cancer.

I remember listening to Luke-O talk, in amazement. He was five years younger than I but had the wisdom that was otherworldly. He was having so much fun, as if his body was not a hindrance or inconvenience, and it never stopped him from having a full life until his last day. Luke-O passed peacefully at the age of twenty-one. That young man was wise beyond his years and blessed beyond his body.

Living a full life is incredibly reliant on your ability to

reframe the hand you've been dealt. Everyone is given this opportunity. We cannot control what happens to us in life but we can control how we react to it. It's all we've got. It's what we can control. To master reframing, you can turn anything that happens to you into something that empowers you.

I will explain in the Alignment Pillar how your soul spends most of your life just learning and figuring out how to use this body, mind, and heart. For this Integration chapter, I want to teach you that integrity is about getting the mind and mindset intact to lead a great life. This includes forgiveness, and it is not about the old adage, 'forgive and forget.'

Forgiveness has two factors: acceptance and release. You cannot forgive or forget if you refuse to accept that what happened, happened. If you spend your life in judgment, such as blame, shame, hatred, resentment, revenge, envy, and more, you will stay locked in your suffering, confusion, and pain.

In the example I chose earlier, I work ever so gently with humans processing sexual abuse to help them accept what happened to them. This can be painful in the moment because they have spent so much of their lives resisting and resenting that they have been violated. It is our own judgment of ourselves that prevents our progress as much as our blame of others. I help them get clear about what happened by going over the facts vs the interpretations of the facts. When I ask my client to tell me what happened, we identify every step of the story as a fact or an interpretation and this helps them to sort out which is which. This can be challenging to do alone and I suggest a trusted individual, specifically a professional, to support you in trying this out.

There is often a lot of conversation, crying, and realizations that occur at this time, and we do not move forward in the work until the client can acknowledge that they accept that this has happened to them. A key note on forgiveness is that you cannot release what you refuse to accept. You cannot lose something you never had. You cannot fail at something you never try, but you also miss out on the freedom available from the process of acceptance.

The beautiful part that I am excited to share with you, is that it is nearly instantaneous. Once someone can accept what has happened to them, they can choose to release it. This happens like a sunrise. As we work our way through a completion and forgiveness conversation, the darkness of night begins to fade. The sky becomes lighter and lighter until the first ray of sun peaks over the horizon. In that exact moment, the resistance to the thing has been dropped, therefore, the image in the mind shifts, and so does the projection of it on our life. All of a sudden, you can see every way of being associated with the old projection. The same way the sun brings everything into view, so does acceptance. You can see relationships and circumstances set up by that projection, and realize it is not who you truly are at all. This is the pivotal point, when you become at choice about your circumstance and can choose to release it.

Fair warning, some choose to hang onto it. This simply shows that there is more to accept, which is natural. Completion is a process that takes time. These exercises are intended to accelerate that process, but do not expect this to be an overnight cure. Sometimes you get the whole root, sometimes you pull too hard and fast. In any sense, this is progress, and provides a great deal of relief and hope about your future.

Releasing takes on many forms. Here are a few examples to start with:

- Speaking or announcing what you are releasing out loud, as to feel it come out of your body.
- Journaling to keep or writing to burn.
- Meditation and breathwork exercises to alchemize the energy. (Highly recommend Vipassana)
- Art to express the feelings felt and/or freedom created.
- Exercise or movement as to exorcise the stagnant energy that has been lodged within you.
- Acknowledging of the self and announcing release of judgment and the act of forgiving.
- Acknowledging of the other(s) and announcing release of judgment and the act of forgiving.
- Acknowledging of the Higher Power and announcing release of judgment and the act of forgiving.
- Communication of forgiveness with others.
- Celebration of newly created freedom and the courage it took to do the work.
- Many more, get creative! Just let go!

Once you have truly accepted and released, you will feel and know that you have practiced true forgiveness. You will feel it in the framework of your body. For some assistance on this work and to practice with a guided exercise, listen to episode #076 of my Hearts Unleashed Podcast, Two Factors to Forgiveness.

By creating the personal experience of forgiveness, you will then have a true understanding of integration. You will sense the difference between going through the motions of 'forgive and forget' and the actual work of alchemizing judgment back into love. This is the difference between burning a bundle of sage and knowing how to clear energies. It is the difference between owning a deck of tarot cards and understanding how to receive their messages. Forgiveness is a concept. It does not apply until you internalize it. Own it. Integrate it. Integration is *the key* to any and all of this working for you, because that which you know doesn't serve you unless you apply it with intention.

I have spent a large portion of the Integrity Pillar showing you sides of yourself that you may not have seen, fully understood, or heard articulated in such a way. My commitment in this pillar is to create an abundance of awareness and responsibility, so that you realize you are one hundred percent at choice about the quality and direction of your life, the impact that you make, and the legacy that you leave.

Part of creating that awareness is shining light into the shadows. Integration is bringing the shadow side of yourself to light in such a way that you can function fully with every single part of you. I personally have a tattoo on my left wrist that represents dancing with every single part of myself. It reminds me that I have one soul, and many identities of my ego. It helps me to stay in the driver's seat of my life instead of letting one of my egos drive us too far off track. Some of the egos include my inner children, past selves, future selves, my dark sides, my joy and bliss, my excellence, character versions of me, and many more. To recognize that none of them are you without the entire collection is to respect the totality of who you are as an energetic being having a human experience.

So far in this book, I have not referred to the 'shadow self' much. Your shadow is simply made up of the parts of you that you either haven't met yet, or you purposely look away, hide, judge or even try to rid yourself of. So far, the example has been the darkness of trauma. There are other, more natural parts of you that you may be embarrassed of or feel threatened by. These are all parts of you that you have to learn to accept, love, and even share them. Integration is learning how to share them in such a way that they facilitate you being empowered in your life and empowering others. Never forget that acceptance and integration are the keys to your freedom.

My favorite example of this is being a nudist. I personally love being nude. I love my body. I appreciate my body as the home of my soul and I love expressing myself in that way. Before fully understanding this, I would judge myself as immature, weird, strange, perverted, overly sexual, an attention whore, and so much more. I realized it didn't bother me as a college athlete where it was natural and predictable. Once entering adulthood, I didn't have the same relationship to it. I only saw it as sexual, and even if it isn't always about sexuality to me, I simply did not give that part of myself attention for many years.

Before accepting this underdeveloped part of myself, I didn't necessarily see it as an authentic expression of my being. I saw it as a dysfunctional part of my personality. I thought there was something wrong with me.

Specifically in reference to my chosen career paths of teacher, coach, public speaker, and author, I thought there was a certain identity that I must live up to as appropriate, politically correct, morally sound, and more. I feared people would judge me as a bad influence that promotes perversion. Through the process of exploring my body, and loving it with grace and gentle kindness, I saw how I was living by someone else's definition of appropriate. When my internal projection changed, so did my reality, and my relationship to nudity. I immediately realized how much I appreciate others' bodies and their sensual self-expression. I suddenly understood that I follow leaders on social media who take ownership for and embody their self-love, and that it inspired me. I then started to see myself as one of them. This was a beautiful shift for me, because I granted myself my own permission to love my body and to be at ease with my comfort around nudity.

Over the course of exploring my love of being nude, I also explored what it looked like to share that and express it. I practiced dancing in front of the mirror. I practiced being naked outside, in designated areas of course. I practiced sharing it with others (the concept, not my body) and it was widely accepted. The same way other leaders influenced me, I found out that I was inspiring others who shared their stories of body shame, and how I inspired their body acceptance and exploration. I will never forget that a friend messaged me to share that she had taken on her own nude mirror work after hearing one of my shares and had healed a long-open wound by reconnecting with her body.

It felt fulfilling to take the chance of sharing my true self and finding out that my vulnerability had made a difference for another. It was worth moving far beyond fear and judgment of my personal preferences to get to experience empowering others in such an important way. This is my personal favorite example and I hope you receive the message that it is safe to be you. It is a narrative of our past projections that it is unsafe to be open, raw, real, vulnerable, and unapologetic. It is safe to be all of you, and many (most) people will love and prefer the realest you that you have to offer.

An added benefit: the breakthrough is that in accepting my nudism, I have become bolder in dozens of other areas of life. *That* is what I mean by learning to integrate your shadow. You are creating a natural momentum of courage in your life because proving to yourself that living authentically will not kill or destroy you will have you showing up powerfully time and time again. It will have you more willing to discover other parts of you, that you didn't know were there. This will lead you toward your totality. This will lead to you feeling whole and complete, and when you do, you will be experiencing yourself as an alchemist.

If you know how to use a stove, you can feed yourself for life. If you can master your egos, you can be versatile instead of volatile and enjoy the variety of life. This naturally heals your relationship to your worth, intuition, and capability. This is the development of emotional intelligence and as a result, your frequency will keep spiraling upward. This adds momentum to the Cycle of Love. More specifically, it will feel like the Cycle of *Self*-Love, and the destination is Transformation Station.

I have been explaining transformation throughout this book, and I want to clarify that the ultimate threshold and last stage of it is Transcendence. The guidance for this book is meant to lay out the path toward Transcendence. Many people also call this enlightenment and some people get distracted, overwhelmed, or turned off by that concept.

To be clear, for as long as you can reference this book, you will be in your human form. You will have judgment. You will have egos. You will live on this plane and be of this plane. That means you will have normal human needs that require materials, money, and the other contracts of humanity's modes of operation. I was guided to teach you about and lead you towards

Transcendence in a form applicable to everyday living in modern society. I am not expecting you to become a monk or a nun. I am not encouraging you to donate all of your belongings, leave your family, and become a disciple of anyone. We don't need more gurus sitting in monasteries - we need leaders of the free world facilitating love, compassion, and change amongst us. I am inviting you to transcend your humanness enough to live and lead fully instead of floundering in the distractions this world has to offer.

The next two pillars, Alignment and Faith, will most definitely be about transcending your humanness. Integrity is very human based. It's very materialistic. It's very purposeful and strategic. In the Alignment and Faith Pillars, we will talk about soul much more than strategy. To wrap up this chapter about integrity, I want to bring back that last stage of transformation: Transcendence.

At this stage of transformation, the skill is to be the most absolute, unapologetic, unabashed, unleashed version of yourself anywhere, at any time, with anyone, about anything. Let's be particular about what I mean here. This isn't about walking around with two middle fingers up to anyone who has powerful reflection and feedback for you. This is about full-scale integration. This is about recognizing all the parts of you and accepting them fully. It is about exploring the depths of your heart, and grounding into your intuition with certainty, clarity, and faith. Existing at this stage of transformation is about not being detoured by doubt, distraction, challenge, or resistance.

This level of transformation is about being so sure and certain about who you are as an energetic being that *nobody* can tell you about yourself! *Nobody* can shift your relationship with yourself. This isn't about arrogance; it is about being rooted in a truth that only your own inner work can reveal to you. It is arriving at a sense of peace with who you are instead of feeling some inherent need to fix or change yourself. Not to be confused with natural evolution that will occur, accepting your full self will grant you access to fully accepting everyone else. When you are able to integrate this knowledge with the humility of transformation, you will feel steadfast in your purpose, focus, and direction. It is an incredible sight to see someone faithfully on fire about what they came here to do and follow that inner guidance boldly.

In this first half of the book, we have walked through the work of self discovery, self development, and self mastery. This naturally invites you into the stage of complete and utter self-acceptance. This is where you transcend your humanness and integrate the energetic version of you with the material version of you. This is where you put your feet on the ground and start taking steps in your contribution to humanity as the authentic leader that you are. At this stage, you are able to see, own, and share any part of you that you may discover from this point forward.

As we transition into the next part of this book, I invite you to shift from any egocentric perspective and into your energetic being; the soul of who you are. What is available by taking on integrity is your fulfillment of your soul's purpose on this planet. Integrity is about getting all of your affairs in order, taking full responsibility for your impact, and completing your past in such a way that you set yourself free.

So practice releasing your identity as solely you. We are going to close the gaps of separation so that you may lean into your calling, passion, mission, message, and purpose. We will clear as much gunk as possible so that you can be all of you anywhere, at any time, with anyone, about anything. Keep reciting that. Turn it into a tune and it will become the tone of your life. Nothing will be able to stop you. Nothing will be able to deter you. You will be so clear, that any perceived threat or setback is simply an invitation to grow, evolve, and alchemize anything that you encounter back into love, swiftly and quickly.

Once you do this, you are free to make the biggest difference you are called to make in your life. You will be energetically available to honor the divine guidance that you receive. Something I want you to keep in mind about this work is that when you master yourself, you master the human psyche. If you examine yourself enough, you will be able to draw natural conclusions about human patterns that keep us trapped. This is a gift of the work and is only available through your own singular transformation. This isn't knowledge to study, it is wisdom to ascertain, and then create an impact on others by nature of you being an example of the work.

As a result of your own integrity, alignment, and faith, you will understand the human condition and how to fully own your role as an alchemist. This is one of your greatest gifts, as you will become a beacon of hope, light, love, and compassion in the world. You will draw people in. You will be able to transmute anything back into love in such a way that people will request your mentorship in creating their own peace and alignment. You will naturally evolve into your personal expression of leadership and craft your own process to teach the magic of alchemy, because as you now know; when you take the magic and mysticism out of alchemy to understand the methodology, you can understand the mechanics enough to bring the magic back. It's time to bring the magic back.

Alignment Pillar

Chapter 10

Understanding Frequency

Where we are, in the twenty-first century, frequency is becoming a household conversation. Previously considered a scholarly, spiritual, or hippy-dippy topic, frequency is being used on a more mainstream level, and this is important for humanity and the planet. The concept and comprehension of frequency has been around for centuries, but in the Information Age, a time widely known as The Great Awakening, people are becoming more apt to pay attention to what it actually means.

In general, frequency is a measurement of how rapidly the molecules of something are vibrating, and consequently, how they take form on this plane. Everything is frequency made up of a collection of molecules and atoms that are vibrating and regenerating at a higher or lower rate. Some vibrate slower; therefore, they make up more dense materials in this field. They take shape as inanimate, physical objects that we see, touch, taste, smell, feel, and use. Some are faster and less dense, and they constitute a human body, animal, or other living objects that grow and reproduce. Some are even less dense, and they formulate water, air, light and more. Some are so light and rapid that they cannot be detected by the human senses.

For frequencies higher than the physical senses, you must rely on your intangible senses; mental, emotional, and spiritual. Examples of these are the concepts of love, time, currency, intuition, and possibility. You have to be able to use your energetic senses as signal receptors the same way that you might feel around a dark room as to not trip over the coffee table. It is in its theoretical nature, where the concept of frequency has previously gotten lost in translation for the mainstream folks. People who require seeing to believe will be limited in what they have access to when creating their life to be an abundant one.

We can intellectually acknowledge that just because we cannot physically see, handle, or manipulate something doesn't mean it isn't real. We can say that and feel confident about accepting abstract concepts. However, when it comes to applying that to our lives, we default to what we know. Combined with the fact that we didn't attend Hogwarts, we feel powerless in using the magic of frequency to manifest miracles in our lives...or at least that is how many of us relate to it.

The understanding and skills of frequency were not taught and nurtured in the educational system, and as I mentioned in the last pillar, we judge what we don't understand. The power available in comprehension of frequencies has been grossly underutilized, simply because of a lack of understanding and a desire for control. Everyone operating from their own inner authority is threatening to anyone trying to maintain a sense of authority. This 'seems' dangerous to the constructs of society but consider that those constructs are not for the highest good of all. Since we have been limited in our education, the interest in and mastery of frequency has been scoffed at as silly, pretend, witchcraft, or magic. As a result, it is also seen as an unreliable, unpredictable, and irresponsible method of operation for sustainable and duplicable success. This is not because it is fake or useless. It is because it is powerful beyond measure or control.

You may have noticed the overall intelligence and communication of humanity rising in this Information Age. That is because more people are opening their hearts and minds to trust and surrender to a truth that cannot be manipulated on this plane. I explained how taking the magic out makes sense of all this work. I will keep explaining these abstract concepts to you, in an effort to assist you in making sense of them. I also invite you to soften your heart to the idea that you have always known how to manage frequency on a cellular level. It is second nature for you, so there is more unlearning to do than learning. You must drop your disbelief, and you will find that recognition and faith exist right under the surface of how you have been trained to be and think. You have been using frequency and the Law of Attraction your entire life without fully knowing what you are doing, and I am simply training you how to use it on purpose and with purpose.

Mental health and emotional intelligence are becoming more important by the day, because we are beginning to recognize it as the root cause of humanity's issues. We are also witnessing how some of those who have mastered frequency and the human psyche are not using it for the good of all. Harnessing and alchemizing energy wasn't always popular, because not enough people had it figured out to translate it into layman's terms and tools. This is changing rapidly, and more genuine people are teaching these concepts to empower each other and make sure our brothers and sisters take control of their brains, hearts, and lives.

The frequency of humanity will continue to rise as more of us awaken to our potential as energetic beings having a human experience. No one has authority over you. You have authority over no one. When we diminish any separateness, our potential will become limitless. The tides keep turning us toward atonement for using our free will for singular benefit. When we come together at the frequency of Love, we will be operating in harmonic unison of service and devotion, and that will be the highest frequency we can attain. This may seem daunting and impossible. I am inviting you to start practicing your faith for the remainder of this book.

For a long while, humanity has prioritized egocentric desires, such as looks and material wealth. We have striven to attain lives above our means at the cost of others. I am all for believing in abundance, especially the idea that we don't acquire it from a zero-sum game that denies others basic human necessities, freedoms, and rights. We have negotiated our integrity and dignity for what appears successful and prosperous. This is a low and unsustainable frequency to exist at as a species.

This has created such havoc that people are waking up to the fact that you can have the entire outward appearance of a great life and feel energetically poor, exhausted, and unfulfilled. We are also waking up to the fact that our level of consumption is negatively affecting the planet and the entire ecosystem reliant upon it. We have maxed out on commercial consumerism so much that we are finally able to conclude that it is not the end-all-be-all key to happiness, peace, and purpose. As more have woken up to this, they have begun searching for meaning beyond the physical representations. With enough consistent commitment, anyone can find what they are seeking in the energetic realm. The best part of this is that we don't have to go searching far to find exactly what we are seeking.

Do you know where you have access to the energetic realms? From within.

That's right, my friend. What will make you the most deeply satisfied on a soul level is honoring your soul. Like, duh. We know this. We just haven't been taught how to prioritize or apply this awareness. In this Alignment Pillar, I am asking you to loosen your grip on the material realm and open up to the idea that your happiness lies beyond the physical boundaries of this world.

If happiness is a feeling, then it will require a different means of acquisition than something physical. News flash: happiness is a frequency. Much like you might need a stepstool to get something off the top shelf, you need to elevate to a higher frequency to experience the higher orders of emotion and intellect. To reach those top shelf frequencies, your step stool is honoring your soul, which entails tuning into your own authentic frequency. I will teach you how to do that.

Over the years, this is why therapy, recovery, support, ministry, mediation, coaching, mentorship, and many other forms of self-growth have become more popular. School did not teach mental health, emotional intelligence, or spiritual connection, and so those who have figured it out have taken on teaching it outside of the constructs of institutionalized education. This wave has caught momentum over the decades and won't be stopped from turning the tides of humanity from competition to collaboration.

The highest vibration is Love. That is why I explain how the source of any and all is Love, and why the goal is to guide you back to it. If you can access the highest frequency, you can basically upcycle anything to a higher frequency and alchemize lower order manifestations. This is valuable for the same reason it is not great to be a hoarder. If you never clean your space, you will be bogged down by an overwhelming number of things. Much of it will get forgotten and likely rot, deteriorate, expire, and spoil. This causes problems when wanting to live at a high frequency, because your space is so densely packed with things that no longer serve you and now limit you. To cleanse and alchemize is to release and make space for new. What awaits you is higher frequency, blessings, and prosperity.

As you have read in the Integrity Pillar, there must be awareness, acceptance, and release in the process of transformation for lasting change to take root. We must till the soil of our hearts for it to be fertile for new seed and growth. In reference to our judgment tree, pruning trims the old off and leaves you feeling fresh and strong; similar to how a fresh haircut makes you feel like a new human. Cut off the dead ends, trim the fat, out with the old, my friend! I can say it about a thousand different ways, but the contents of this book will do nothing for you if you are not applying them to your life. This book will not change your life, these words will guide you to change your life.

So, let's start talking about strategy. I'd like to teach you how you can change your frequency and therefore, your life. This book is a guide back to love, so I will give you even more guidance details in this Alignment Pillar. This is a fascinating pillar, because as mentioned early in the book; alignment is where integrity and faith collide.

If Love is the source of all, faith is the spigot, alignment is the hose, and integrity is whatever is being watered with love. This pillar is a conduit for faith and love to manifest in this world. Your job is to be in alignment as often as possible and get back into alignment quickly and swiftly. Your level of transformation will shift this from a baby giraffe stumbling and learning to walk, to a cheetah sprinting with grace and agility. I will give you everything I know to support your consistent alignment, and you will begin to see things manifesting at that astonishing cheetah speed.

The chapters of this pillar are written to lift you higher than this realm of physical reality into the energetic realm where love resides. Intentions of this pillar are to open doors, shine light, facilitate flow, and stir energy, so that you will feel guided directly back to love. When it comes down to a conversation of frequency, this pillar is about learning how to raise and maintain it. The themes of this pillar are the elevation and activation of your soul self. I will guide you to soul resonance so that you may collude with your internal guidance system. The purpose of the information and instruction in this section is to teach you to co-create with God and the Universe as the energetic being you are.

You came to this planet with a divine purpose. You chose to come here. Remember, you saw the docket and agreed to this journey. Agreeing to be in alignment is stepping into a river of abundance and letting it take you downstream, effortlessly.

In my times of resistance and questioning my path, I have heard God say, "relax child, for you cannot possibly imagine what I have planned for you." I would get a very clear sense that it was not only for the highest good of all but was also leading me to a far better life than I could have ever planned for. God has in store for us levels of abundance that we could never force our hand at creating.

As the divine masculine energy, God is a provider. If we will only follow his will and surrender the visions of our ego, we will not only be led to our greatest life; getting there will be absolutely effortless. However, the effort you will experience as a human will be in the surrendering to follow and receive. We have not learned these skills and they will feel new and scary. I will provide all of the guidance I have available to you for you to practice the art of surrender and flow. This is your invitation to step into the stream of infinite consciousness. Everything you need is there and available directly to you. This is relaxing into the frequency of Love.

In order to relax into the highest frequency, you must stop tuning into frequencies that are not your own. This includes those of others, things, circumstances, your ego, and lower order emotions. I have already shared a lot about this, and I will conclude this thought by saying that the most important frequency for you on the planet is the one in your body; your own personal frequency.

The best way to sense this frequency is by being the most still and quiet you can be. Then, once in that state, you can begin training your inner ear to hear your body communicating to you and train your inner eye to see what it is showing you. I am a visual, audible, and kinesthetic learner, so tangible examples help me connect to my personal frequency. Quieting the outside world to tune into my inner world shows me how I am actually feeling very quickly.

On any given day, if I tune into my body and identify the emotions percolating, then I can begin alchemizing them back to love. If I am experiencing sadness, I observe it and let it be, as to simply witness it. When I witness it without a desire to fix or change it, I can detect its cause and simply be with the pain. Allowing the pain will also allow it to pass through without much turmoil.

To describe this in another way: there is the emotion of sadness, and then there is our reaction to the emotion of sadness. This is like the pain of having a sliver in your finger *and* the compounded reaction to the pain. To effectively move through any emotion, it is best to practice not having the second reaction. This may come as a shock to some, but the second reaction is optional. Not reacting to pain (and pleasure) is an age-old practice of the Buddhists and is their key to transcending suffering. Feel it. Allow it. Let it be and let it go.

If you can master this, you will experience a great sense of freedom and relief. Allowing thoughts, feelings, and emotions to be fully present will naturally alchemize them, because you are no longer judging or resisting them. When you allow an emotion to surface and actually watch it like a student, you can learn from it. You can hear what it is communicating, honor it, and, if necessary, follow through with the communication.

When we become willing to feel our feelings, we are able to move through them in new ways. Remember, what you resist, persists. Our inability to be with our pain, suffering, dark thoughts, and judgments is what keeps them around, screaming for attention. To transmute a persistent or nagging energy pang, focus on it. Allow it to be around. Give it your attention. It is communicating a need that you have been ignoring. To receive the communication will transmute its need to be seen, felt, and heard.

My favorite example of this is anger. Anger is a signal from our body that serves as a survival mechanism. When anger is present, there is also a threat being *perceived* by the body; key word here being perceived. Anger is a judgment of things being unjust, unfair, hurtful, inconsiderate, and more. Anger signals a need to protect, attack, lash out, fight, resist, and more. Without an ability to observe our anger, we are simply being run by it. With our willingness to observe our anger, we may witness, accept, and transmute it into something more powerful.

This turns *us* into something more powerful. It transmutes us into *someone* more powerful. Reflecting back to our conversation about impact, this turns us into a radiant being that vibrates at a consistently high frequency, acting as a beacon for others seeking the light. This is a great segue into explaining the ability to read the energy of others. I was just sharing about tuning into your own frequency by going inward. I want to normalize for you exactly how good you are at reading energy so you can use the skill you already have.

When you walk into a room, you can pick up on the energy right away. When you walk up on a grumpy gills, you can sense their ho-hum attitude immediately. When you meet someone clean and clear, they shine like a penny. You can sense frequency easily. You have this skill so it will behoove you to use this more intentionally.

For starters, it is time for you to be tuning into your own energy more frequently. For this, I suggest meditation, mirror work, and journaling. These are three mediums that involve you just being with you. Meditation is widely accepted as access to the higher frequencies and if you think about it, the point of meditation on this plane is to sit so still as to transcend your physicality. The objective is to project your perception into a realm that doesn't have shape, form, constructs, limitations, or boundaries. Dwelling in boundlessness will have you vibing highly, in order to come back to your body clear and inspired.

Mirror work is to witness the way you wear your vibe in and on your body. The look in your eyes, your posture, your aura, and mannerisms all reveal your energy. Studying your own body language and having intentional conversations with yourself in your different energies will empower you to identify and transmute more efficiently. This is powerful when mastered, because you never have to stay anchored into low energy for more than a few seconds or minutes of processing. This can get you back into your leadership anywhere, at any time, around anyone, about anything, and that is alchemy in action.

Journaling is powerful due to the effect of language. Not all of us can hear the communications of our souls in a super direct way. I often guide clients through meditations to receive messages from their soul, spirit guides, guardian angels, ancestors, and passed loved ones. I smile lovingly when we both have our eyes closed and

I instruct them to listen, and they inform me in a disappointed fashion, "I can't hear anything." I know that this is a matter of alignment, and that it is perfectly fine. Journaling is a powerful tool to strengthen the muscle of hearing from within. Our soul, hand, and pen will conspire without the interference of our brain if we let the ink just glide across the paper without much thought. Our inner messages will be revealed if we dedicate ourselves to a consistent journaling practice which will contribute to the development of our meditation and mirror work practices.

All of these practices combined will set us free to see and hear our frequencies and receive guidance from within. You have to be able to drop your physical barriers to access your ethereal self; your energetic body. Tuning into yourself will show you where you are, and training on your own will help you tremendously when you are out in the world and your frequency is being impacted by other forces.

Maintaining high frequency is a skill, like anything else. It takes awareness, commitment, and practice. You *can* and *will* become good at it and being able to hang out at a high vibe will attract all of the goodness you could ever imagine. Maintaining high frequency is also about alchemizing low frequency when you encounter it. I will teach you the mechanics of alchemizing energies later in this pillar, so buckle up, baby.

On a personal level, this is about observing your internal state with the tools I just shared. Out in the world with others, this is about being able to hold space for their frequency without letting it attach to you in such a way that it acts like an anchor to your soul. Instead, you will be empowered to lift others up by helping them be with, process, and transmute their energy to higher frequencies.

This is the work of an alchemist. This work is absolute magic, and I am so excited for you to get to experience it from your new levels of awareness. You are an alchemist, my love. Own it. Love it. Be it. In this pillar, I plan to teach you exactly how to do that.

Chapter 11

Distinguishing Dimensions

I am going to carry over our conversation about frequency into a lesson about the different energetic dimensions we have access to. I have mentioned how frequency can go seen and unseen, but I want you to know that you have access to the various levels at all times if you are willing to train yourself to raise your vibration. The same way it is important to train to run a marathon, it is important to train your head and heart to make it to the finish line of transformation. Granted, growth will be a lifelong journey. That being said, 'the struggle' most people suffer through on a daily basis *can* and *will* end if you are committed to existing at a high vibration. This gets really fun, because even when challenging things happen to someone who is constantly vibing high, they are less impacted by adversity. If you are healthy, well, and empowered, judgment doesn't penetrate you the same way, because you aren't absorbing everyone's shame, guilt, and negative energy. Other people's projections bounce right off when you are elevated and clear about yourself and your life.

Transformation is not about constant sunshine and rainbows. Life on Earth will always present us with challenges, trials, and tribulations. Being transformed is about being able to transcend above adversity, fast and frequently. That means that you are living empowered upwards of ninety percent of the time. There is no doubt your humanness will swirl you into some low vibe feelings and experiences. Being transformed means that you have the awareness and ability to transmute those energies back to love. Even the most challenging times are intentional and have purpose - to help you hone your gifts and skills of alchemy. If you remember this, nothing can break you.

Understanding the third, fourth, and fifth dimensions will certainly help you transcend your experiences in the third dimension with ease and grace. I want to be super clear that what I am teaching you is all about integration of this information. I do *not* teach this information so that you can peace out of this plane, move to the mountains, go off the grid, start a commune, and never engage with civilization again. I am committed to sharing this information to empower you as the leader that you are *in* the Collective of humanity. We need you. We need each other.

It is not by avoiding and ignoring each other that we will heal. It is through interdependence that we will thrive. There are four types of dependence to understand about in this life. The first type of dependence is genuine reliance, for example, a newborn baby or an elderly person. This is the 'if you don't feed and care for me, I will die' kind of dependence. Then, there is codependence, which we are aware of, but all too unfamiliar with. This kind of dependence can sound like 'I lean on you and if you leave, I will lose my balance until something or someone new picks me up.' This is the silent killer of humanity's true atonement and freedom. We are reliant on each other for things that we should be doing and handling ourselves. Codependency is disempowering to all of us, and without studying it more seriously, we will never fully understand all the ways we sabotage ourselves, our relationships, and our loved ones.

The next is independence. I have a special place in my heart for independence, because when I see someone committed to independence, I see their commitment to the greater good developing. Beware, we often choose this level of dependence out of spite, hurt, loneliness, resentment, fear and more but it *is* an initiation out of codependency and into interdependence. This stage is interesting because we are wrestling the most with standing on our own, as well as the fact that our insecurities, trauma, and trust issues are on display. This is the most important time to dive into the inner work of transformation. Doing so will help us level up to the next stage of dependence.

The last type, interdependence, cannot occur out of this order. None of them can. You must graduate from one to the other in the sequence that I introduced.

I don't say *must* as if someone will force you through each one and give you a badge at each graduation. I am saying that life will take you through these stages naturally. Something that will happen is that as you practice independence, you will slip into codependent behaviors. As you practice interdependence, you will catch yourself protecting yourself with independent reflexes. This is okay and natural while you strengthen your skills along with your maturation and development.

Interdependence is the concept that 'we are better together.' This means that independent people actively choose to engage with other independent people and collaborate, with a commitment to the highest good of all. If someone reaches interdependence as an adult, at the time of being a dependent elder they will still be interdependent, because they will have wisdom to offer those who care for them.

In the Western world, we have gotten away from respecting our elders. There are a variety of reasons for this, ranging from economical to spiritual. A large factor is attributed to the reality that large portions of previous generations did not work their way past codependence. They did not have the services available that we do, and 'mental health' carried more of a stigma

It was not as common for people to get help and those that did often took the route of religion or counseling, both of which treated the symptom more often than the cause in the earlier years of self development. Along with the evolution of humanity, the mental and emotional health industry has evolved to support this shift. When a codependent elder shifts into a reliant state of being, this can be a heavy experience for a family, which can naturally lead to tensions and resentments. This is no one's fault per say, but it does require Transcendence to gain clarity about the situation so that the people involved can feel empowered and at choice about the situation.

In any case of an unhealthy dependency, it can be confusing for emotionally immature adults to collaborate when one or all are simply projecting on each other with little understanding of what is happening. Understanding this can also help us care for one another more effectively. Knowing this information will help us break generational patterns of passing down trauma.

At lower frequencies, people compete to beat. They do unto others what has been done to them. Hurt people hurt people and contribute to that Cycle of Hurt practically unconsciously. Dependent, codependent, and even independent people withhold abundance from each other as if there is a limit to it and begin to hoard. People who struggle with dependency and codependency are not present to their own capabilities and gifts that they have to offer, therefore, they are incredibly reliant on others to care for and provide for them. They are takers and this can exhaust valuable resources of humankind. Not helping this population grow is detrimental to their connection to a Higher Power, which prevents them from fulfilling their purpose on the planet. This is why it is so important to become the leaders that we are, because empowering ourselves and each other empowers our evolution and begins to naturally dissolve our barriers to success.

When people are simply left to operate at these low frequencies, they repel others from them. People who operate at these levels, especially in their adult years, are engulfed in judgment and stuck in this three dimensional reality, as if this is all there is. It is toxic, disheartening, and demoralizing to exist in this frequency for years or decades. Individually, we act as if we can just leave these people behind, and in some sense, we must. Transformation must be an individual choice on each person's part. However, we must be prepared to guide these beautiful souls when they awaken to their true nature. It is so important to teach this information so that people can actually be at choice about in which dimension they exist and have the freedom to choose their way out of misery if they wish.

That being said, the way out of the low order of dependence is to recognize the other dimensions, which I will explain in depth here in a minute. I first want to share that independence is much in the realm of the fourth dimension and interdependence is the fifth. As you can sense, the higher you climb, the freer you get to be. The higher you elevate, the more connected you are. The more connected you are, the more separation and judgment will fall away, leaving true, authentic connection possible and available.

When we create our world to have real connection, we have the potential to realign more and more people who have strayed off track from the core of who they really are; love. That is why I need you here. We are better together. We came to this planet *for* this work. Our souls took a body to usher in an era of love and transcendence. In the example of Adam and Eve, the Garden of Eden was a place of purity and abundance. There was no lack or need. Just bliss, coexistence, and love. It was our humanness and free will that caused our fall from grace, and it is our free will that will get us back to a more peaceful time for humanity. We must choose to be leaders of love. We must choose to step up as guides for each other, and interdependence will afford us the opportunity to collaborate on our arrival back to peace.

A dear friend refers to our atonement, or our arrival back to purity as 'The Garden State,' and I think it is a brilliant reference. To walk each other 'home' to our innocence will require each and every one of us to accept our role and responsibility to be accountable to ourselves, our word, each other, and the Collective. This will bring us peace. Judgment will keep us divided. Interdependence will unite us.

So, as I share these dimensions, I want to explain why they are so important. As explained above, they are our access to love and innocence. They are our pathway to peace. This visible, material reality is not all there is, and trusting in the unseen will manifest things out of thin air to come straight to you. This is important for your leadership. This is vital to be your fullest self and live your fullest life. This is essential to our salvation.

I would like to start explaining the dimensions by

breaking them down in relation to this book; the third dimension is the pillar of integrity, fourth dimension is alignment, and the fifth is faith.

I say that the Integrity Pillar represents the third dimension because this dimension is about the tangible, physical realm here in the Universe. It is measured by height, width, and depth. It is comprised of what we can see and perceive with our human senses, including what is on the ground and in the sky. It is what we can see, touch, hold, and feel - including this book - all the way up to the stars and planets.

This also relates to the cognitive concepts of human consciousness, such as math, science, history, and politics. Integrity is about being your word, and our word is of this realm. Words are something the human mind created to shape thought energy on this planet. We have shaped things into form with our language and our ability to articulate our thoughts, feelings, and intellect.

Integrity is about having your life in working order, and that is primarily an effect of handling your business here in this life. Having an orderly room and car, paying bills on time, hitting deadlines, having a healthy body and relationships are all actions and results of integrity. These actions keep us grounded here on Earth and make way for our connection to the fourth dimension. If we are out of integrity and have a disorderly life, we are distracted, distraught, and bogged down by this 3D, material world, and have very little wherewithal to believe in or access higher vibrations that will bring us the relief and joy we so desperately desire.

Many confuse this physical realm for all that there is and feel gridlocked into life. It is those that only believe in what they see that struggle with what they see. It is being able to transcend this physical reality that sets you free from feeling stuck in your circumstances. If you are reading this book, I assume that you already believe there are more forces at play than just what you see here in this lifetime.

Transcending the 3D to enter the 4D is basically understanding abstract concepts such as time, currency, rules, and creativity. I share that this dimension is reflective of the Alignment Pillar because your physical 3D reality is based on what you align yourself with in the 4D. To believe the idea that all you see is all there is, limits what is possible for you. If you operate from this limited perspective, you have no facility with your abstract imagination to bring something new to your life. This can be challenging, disheartening, and demoralizing over time.

The fourth dimension is where time bends, rules are relative, success is highly attainable, and abundance is so available. There are fewer boundaries and constructs in the 4D. Highly successful people in the 3D have access to the 4D, and as a result, they are able to produce much more desirable effects in significantly less time. This is because they are not gridlocked into the reality that others attempt to create for them. People who understand their own power understand that rules and laws of this world are made up. They understand that we humans designed the concept of time to track and measure. They see and sense that currency, politics, and religion were mainly created to conform and institutionalize us. People who get this also get that they have a choice in the matter.

Humans' societal norms, rules of engagement, and expectations of etiquette are all made up by someone's standard modes of operation. Someone established them and received sufficient agreement from others that what they declared was acceptable human behavior. From there, it was taught and handed down as truth and law. Without knowing any better, so many humans have simply accepted the way they were raised and continued this cycle, and the societal norms that have come along with it. Until now, that is.

More than ever, during this Information Age, we are empowered to communicate with others on an incomprehensible scale to expose injustice, institutionalization, and indoctrination. More people are awakening, learning, sharing, and teaching as to awaken more. This is why we need you. This is the era in which we are truly able and empowered to speak up and out about the fourth dimension, where the seemingly concrete reality of the third dimension crumbles like a soft cookie on a warm day. This is the time of Collective transformation. This is an era of restoration. It is our time to start returning back to love. We must all see, understand, and accept our roles as alchemists as to make our return.

People may come to envy someone tapped into the fourth and fifth dimensions, because they operate much more fluidly. They march to the beat of their own drum and have learned how to win the game of life, and so, they play it to their advantage. There are many people who think they want the image of abundance and success, and yet, aren't willing to get uncomfortable enough to do the inner work necessary to reach that level of achievement. This can become frustrating and triggering for someone who insists this three-dimensional reality is the end-all-be-all when they witness someone transcend their definition of truth and not play by their perceived rules. In terms of alchemizing judgment, it is essential to understand that the frustrations and opinions of those obeying the third dimension restrictions are that they have a deep desire to have the level of freedom they are witnessing and judging. It is about their own craving to do as they please versus conforming to what they were taught.

I will likely not stop emphasizing that this is why your evolution is so important. You will break molds and pave paths that others do not yet have the tools to forge and navigate. Leaders must step up to make way for those willing but confused, ready but unclear, and awakened but scared. It is our duty to shine light on the path until their light grows and shines brightly, too. I explain this in the way that other body positive leaders inspired me to accept my own body and nudity. Imagine what your authentic boldness will inspire others to think, believe, do, and create.

To begin wrapping up my explanation of the fourth dimension, I want to share that the fourth dimension is where creativity, inspiration, and imagination are granted access to enter the third dimension. It is through the cracks in the concrete that brilliance can seep into our physical space. We must be willing to bust up the barriers on our limiting beliefs and disempowering ways in order to receive those hits of intuition and infinite intelligence available to us from the 5D. This is why the fourth dimension is the dimension of alignment. It is our responsibility to align with the highest good to be a channel of love that can flow to, and through us, and enter this 3D field. This is where the magic begins.

We are energetic beings having a human experience. I am going to jump ahead in my description of the fifth dimension to say that the spirit of who we are exists in the 5D. When the soul takes a body here, it cannot relate to the physical challenges we face in this concrete reality. Being on this planet can be a very dense experience without intentionally tapping into the higher frequency planes of existence.

In the fifth dimension, there is no time and space. There is no form, boundary, standard, definition, or construct. There is nothingness. Everything comes from the same source of energy. There is this nucleus at the center of all that is. This nucleus is that core of love energy that I keep referencing. Some relate to it as God or Consciousness or Source Energy. In any sense, when you go there energetically, your human identity dissolves. When you take yourself to that place, you blend with the nucleus energy of all that is. By way of being an energetic being having a human experience, you can choose to opt for the energetic experience. You would not recognize yourself again until you bring yourself back into this 3D reality. When you let your mind and spirit wander, they only take true shape again when you bring them back into your brain and body.

This is important to understand because you are constantly connected to the fifth dimension, and this will begin to make more sense and have more value for you very soon. Because the soul is sourced in a boundless space, when it comes down to Earth to, let's say, 'play human,' it doesn't understand the limitations we are faced with.

You often feel like crap when your brain and heart are constantly pumping brilliant hits of inspiration that you don't feel competent enough to follow through with. You feel anxious and overwhelmed when you can see the visions your spirit is sending you, but you struggle with human fears and insecurities that stop you from taking inspired action to turn those thoughts into things. You overanalyze, rationalize, justify, calculate, and predict yourself right out of courage. As the naturally limited human you are, you resist all those hits with excuses about why you can't be, do, or have what your spirit is nudging you toward. We do this moment to moment. "I can't do that! *Insert limiting belief* Who am I to…. There's no way I could…I am too tired. I am not skilled enough. Nobody will let me…" The reasoning goes on and on with endless justifications. You talk yourself right off the ledge of bravery and slowly tiptoe back to the safety of your comfort zone where your ego has a field day convincing you of the coward that you are.

This is the most prime example of being out of alignment. It is like having your garden hose hooked up to the spigot of faith with a leak gushing out. You are receiving intense amounts of guidance, direction, and urges from your soul, but you are letting them pour onto the ground. This leaves you feeling as if you are a failure for letting your dreams spill out and evaporate.

Before you spiral into hopelessness about all your dreams being dashed into oblivion, allow me to raise the vibe up here. I want you to imagine a golden thread coming from this nucleus of all that is, where your beautiful soul is hanging out. There's this golden thread that pulls through the fourth dimension, down into the third dimension, attached to this little embryo that is you. This little baby growing into the human you will become. This golden thread comes right through the umbilical cord and it gives little baby you life. At our human birth, that umbilical cord is severed and temporarily, so is our direct connection to Infinite Intelligence. At this point, we are disconnected from the source and raised by humans who are likely also disconnected from their source. This is where we are solidified in our 3D reality and the human modes of operation. This is when we are ingrained with concepts of morality, ethics, and integrity per our guardian's definition.

This lasts for as long as it takes for us to awaken. As described earlier, people's awakenings are often traumatic and result in that crumbling effect of their perceived reality. Even if one's awakening is traumatic and painful, it is a blessing. This is when you regain access to your golden thread. When your previous existence is shattered, you naturally begin a search for truth, meaning, and purpose. This is where transformation begins. This is where you begin to hear, see, and sense clear guidance from your soul that actually makes sense, and you are finally willing to follow it.

When you finally accept the invitation to reconnect to that golden thread, you can start tapping into the stream of consciousness flowing through it, coming directly from your soul in the 5D. You can go back to the source. You can visit. You can intentionally channel the brilliance of the love energy. That's where you get your direct downloads for your next inspired actions. That's where everything starts. All of the amazing advances in humanity come from this place. Everything starts as a thought and becomes a thing and thought comes from the nucleus source.

Whatever Higher Power you use to reference it does not matter, because there's no form or definition there. There are no words there. You simply come from it and return to it. It has the same golden thread attached and just shows up as an extension of this Source Energy. I like the idea that you will probably start seeing golden threads everywhere in your life now. I hope you use this visual to solidify your understanding of our true connection and to eliminate your illusion of separateness.

I use this golden thread visual to connect with the person in front of me and the people, places, things, and experiences that I am calling into my life. When I feel called to something, I follow my golden thread back to the source and jiggle the one that I desire. I visualize taking a ride down the golden thread of someone or something else to energetically call them or it closer to myself in the third dimension. Please friend, use this understanding for the highest good of all. Use this visualization to spread love, kindness, blessings, bliss, and joy. The work we are doing in the word is unleashing hearts, not restraining them.

Speaking of unleashing hearts, I would like to take a moment to specifically talk about loved ones passed. Our mortality is only in this third dimension. Our souls return to the source and our golden thread gets reeled back in until a soul decides to take human form again, which is thousands of times per second, in reference to the average birth rate. Souls are enthused to get down here and play human again.

I want to provide this perspective as to support your grieving process and provide an opportunity to gracefully alchemize the human fear and pain of death back into love. Us humans, left behind when a loved one dies, are the ones who recall that human's life. Our brains remember them as the shape, voice, and personality that they were, but when they rejoin that nucleus source, they become a part of you. They reside in the Source Energy. You have access to them on that golden thread. They're everywhere and nowhere because when you head to the core, your identity disappears and you evaporate back into love. It's all the same. You are them. They are you.

That's why I want to encourage you that since

you are in the world right now, to get rid of any b.s. about separation. You are no different than anyone. You are no different than anything and that's why you can attain anything you desire. It is about matching the frequency of whatever you are attempting to access in this physical realm.

Abundance is about understanding that there is no difference between you and a million dollars. There is no difference between you and who you want to spend the rest of your life with. There is no difference between you and anything. If you can go up that thread, tap into the source energy, and truly connect with the frequency of that which you desire, you will attract it in this third dimension with ease, grace, and flow.

This is sincerely beautiful and impactful work to take on. What it requires is you healing every piece of everything that contributes to your separation from all that is. I'm going to wrap up this chapter by showering you with some of my big sis love and ask you to stop believing that you are excluded from access to infinite and unconditional love. You are not that special.

You are not so special that people don't get you, wouldn't understand you, or couldn't love you. Don't do that to yourself. Do not isolate yourself anymore as if you don't belong in this world or nobody wants you. You are loved. You are understood. You are provided for. Everything is available at your choice, to allow yourself to be open to receiving all the blessings that these dimensions have to offer.

Your duty is to get into alignment with the source

of all that is and clear out any gunk blocking your flow along that golden thread. Doing so will create a flow of inspiration and abundance beyond your wildest dreams. You will be free to be, do, and have everything in alignment with your purpose and the highest good of all. I promise you, my friend. What is in alignment with the highest good of all is in your best interest as well. Just keep leaning into the guidance. I am so excited for what's in store for you.

Chapter 12

Know Your Role

We have done a lot of work thus far to clear a path for your purpose on the planet. The Integrity Pillar provided the guidance to clear the gunk, this Alignment Pillar is raising you up, and this chapter is all about identifying your divine role in this lifetime.

Too many beautiful humans with limitless potential get confused about their purpose or role in life being about a title, identity, or position. We use careers to do this. We use our relationships to solidify this. We attach our purpose to our accolades, achievements, impact, and more.

This can be detrimental to our mental and emotional stability over time as these identities come and go. When we put all our eggs in the athlete basket, we suffer an identity crisis post performance peak. When we lean all the way into parenting, we tip over in confusion when our babes take off to start their own lives without us. When we wear our professional title like a badge of honor, we shrink and feel naked or irrelevant without it. It is a slippery slope to identify with anything you can dress up as for Halloween.

Discovering your role in this lifetime usually requires an existential crisis that causes you to start having thoughts like:

- There's got to be more than this!
- There's got to be more to life.
- There's got to be more to me.
- I am bigger than this.
- This can't be it.
- There's no way this is all there is to life.
- I know there is more out there for me.
- I am not fulfilling my potential.
- I am wasting away.
- This isn't what I am supposed to be doing.
- This isn't how I am supposed to be living.
- And so many more…

When we start having these thoughts, feelings, and concerns, it is a sign that we are out of alignment. Whether we understand alignment or not, we naturally set out on a quest to discover the answers to these questions. We crave to resolve these internal issues and begin the journey of transformation.

This is great and exciting, but without some genuine guidance, you may get taken advantage of by a few people looking to make a quick buck off your confusion. I feel incredibly passionate about explaining this situation because of the subtle and predatory way that consumerism thrives on your fears and insecurities.

There are entire businesses and corporations designed to capitalize on a weak human psyche or emotionally undeveloped person.

"Embarrassed about your skin, weight, or body? Buy our miracle oil!"

"Are you sick and tired of your dead-end job? Buy my three-step system to build a six-figure business!"

"Feeling anxious and depressed? Try this drug and feel better instantly without any effort whatsoever!"

"Feeling like an unaccomplished loser? Take my course and you will appear smart and qualified!"

We buy up quick fixes like there's a shortage of them. We are sold on so much garbage that puts us into debt, which sends us deeper into a spiral of misery. This vicious cycle of consumerism to resolve our issues takes us a hundred miles in the wrong direction and causes us to take longer to get back on track. Of course, some of you will read this before making this mistake and still make this mistake. Quite frankly, many people don't learn by hearing or reading or seeing. They learn strictly through the sting of their own experience. In fact, this is how most of us learn our life lessons.

We have to screw things up pretty badly to realize we don't like the position we put ourselves in. Better yet, some people spend a lot of time blaming others for the position they are in, before they ever come around to accepting responsibility for the quality and direction of their life. Don't be that person. You are only extending your suffering and misery.

Instead, let's explore the idea of accelerating this

whole quest for meaning and get to the good stuff. I will tell you; you will still wander off track once or twice, but I would like to help you not get taken advantage of by a snake oil salesman along the way. So while there are no true short cuts through certain initiations in life, you don't have to take the super scenic route to your divine destiny.

I would like to teach you in this chapter to recognize for yourself what it looks and feels like to be in and out of alignment on a moment-to-moment basis. I will teach you a few concepts that you will want to journal, use in mirror work, and meditate on if you are serious about harnessing this skill. Taking this work on in your own life and not just glazing over the words in this book will make the true difference. This awareness doesn't work like osmosis. You must dive into your own consciousness to access your personal answers to these concepts.

In order to recognize when you are off track, you must know what is on track. This means knowing what is most important to you in life. This looks like identifying your core values. I usually suggest anywhere from three to seven, if you're feelin' really passionate. My top core values are authentic connection, hilarious joy, and hearts unleashed. It's that simple.

"But Abigail, you are a coach! Of course you know your core values. You have probably worked on them for ages! I have no idea where to start." It's okay, friend, just breathe. You know your core values. You really do. Your life has been so loud, distracting, and demanding that you haven't been still or quiet enough to recognize them, and that's okay. Today can be that day that you start looking within to discover them. Please note that I said "within." I don't have your core values. Your spouse, parents, children, friends, colleagues, and pastor don't either. You do.

If you choose some to start with and want to change them, you can. They often evolve with you. My core values now were not the same when I was twenty. They may be different in every decade. You are allowed to, and should, revisit them frequently. In fact, it would empower you to internalize them in such a way that you check in with yourself about them multiple times a day. Per choice you make, you have the opportunity to ask yourself, "is this choice in alignment with my core values?"

If you do this, you will develop a quite natural decision making ability that will eliminate a lot of stress and deliberation in your life. Can you imagine what you would do with *all* that energy you gain back from no longer rocking back and forth on the nauseating teeter-totter of indecision? Whew! You will literally gain hours per day back! Yippee for you!

Exploring the idea of establishing core values is super important, valuable, and rewarding, and so is identifying your sense of self. I am loosely referring to the you that is you; your human identity. I say this because we start off with less self-awareness than we think. We are often too critical with ourselves to clearly see and accept ourselves for all of our power, brilliance, beauty, and contribution we have to offer. Mirror work is valuable for meeting the highest version of yourself, because if you sit there long enough and return to the mirror frequently, it is only a matter of time before you start seeing your soul shine through.

As I mentioned in the last chapter, each golden thread is a unique extension of Source Energy. You have your own beautiful expressions of love to share in your time here. That is what I am referencing as your sense of self. Consider what your particular preferences are in expressing love. My sense of self shows up as heart, vitality, power, grace, and light. I bring that brand of love to everything I do and everything I create. If you look at anything that I associate myself with or anything that comes from me, you can see my flavor of love intertwined.

If you inspect your life and observe yourself more consciously, you will be able to identify your brand of love. You will sense your specific expression and impact in this world. This is where you will start to feel a spark of purpose and passion ignite. You will sense some clarity, direction, and motivation because you will know yourself better and feel more confident in what you bring to the world. You will suddenly be standing on the foundation of your own identity, and will realize that the you that you are, can take on *and release* any role you wish.

For example, my sense of self as heart, vitality, power, grace, and light has shown up as:

- Daughter
- Sister
- Athlete

- Student
- Friend
- Girlfriend/Fiancé/Wife
- Teacher
- Manager
- Consultant
- Coach
- Author
- Podcaster/Speaker
- Philanthropist
- CEO
- And more

The *who* that you are will always take precedence over the *whats* that you are. When you respect that fact, you will be free to be fluid in your roles. People, titles, opportunities, and situations can come and go as swiftly as a leaf in the wind, and the idea of loss will no longer take you out of alignment with who you know yourself to be. This is magic, my friend.

This is such a powerful head and heart space to exist from because the next concept I would like to introduce to you is fulfilling your role as a 'cell in the body' of humanity. I love this concept and it has been consistently reliable and useful in my commitment to alignment. For myself, I decided that I am a cell in the spine of the body. I help support the backbone. I keep the body of humanity upright, and my role also extends through the nerves, with a ripple effect to other areas. I also respect that I work in collaboration with other cells in the spine. I am not the only cell, nor am I the whole spine. This helps me stay in my role without envy or urgency, and without feeling isolation.

When making decisions or considering opportunities, I simply ask myself, "is this in my spinal alignment or will this throw my back out?" As a cell in the spine, I am able to easily identify if I am being approached to work with a cell in the brain, hand, or foot. I can quickly determine if something is on my path and will accelerate my journey or take me off track and slow me down. This is quick and clear for me and helps me to conserve my decision making energy for tasks that are in alignment with my role in the spine.

I invite you to consider your role as a cell in the body of humanity. For a bit of perspective, remember that I am saying cell; not whole organ. You are not that special. I say that from love because as important as you are, you are no more important than any other cell. Each and every cell has an important role to play and each role deserves equal respect and dignity.

It is also important to consider that you are *not* that special. I say this just so that you will quit running yourself ragged by being constantly out of integrity and alignment with your specific cell role. I like to remind folks, "ya doin' too much," when they come to me complaining about being exhausted by all the responsibilities they take on, from not simply holding people accountable for their cell roles.

Your need to be needed is killing you. Your unstable need for validation will never be satisfied with your attempts at being important. Your desire to feel relevant is a desperate attempt to prove your worth when there is nothing to prove. Your self-sacrificial martyrdom doesn't make you noble, it deteriorates you. It weakens you as a cell and diminishes your ability to play your singular role to the best of your ability.

It is when we try to be and do it all that we inhibit ourselves and others from fulfilling each unique role. When you relate to others as incapable, you are limiting their range of motion. You are capping their greatness and potential and that is just not nice. Let all the cells shine so that the human body can function fully and thrive completely.

This will be a relief, because you will actually be able to relax like you have been hoping, wishing, and praying for. This might be uncomfortable in the beginning because you have been actively doin' the most for so long, but I promise you, practice makes perfect. The more you relax, the more you get to relax. The relief comes when recognizing that your role in life is super simple, and it is our funny human brains that complicate things. Your purpose here is super simple; live and let live. Love and let love. Be and let be, and be a walking, talking, living, breathing example of love in the world.

You can do it, my dear. I know you can.

So, since you are all clear and inspired about who you are and what you are up to, let's talk about having compassion for those who don't. Before this chapter, you were one of them. Since we are learning to alchemize judgment and all, this seems appropriate.

There are so many people running around this

planet trying everything under the sun to feel a sense of purpose. They chase carrots left, right, up, and down, to no avail. Struggling with a sense of failure, they are also wrapped up in self-hate and judgment for feeling like they don't have a clue about life or happiness. Sprinkle in a little envy over seeing people thriving in their cellular role, and it's a recipe for despair.

Lack of clarity is frustrating, confusing, and discouraging. Try as they might, they may not have resources like this book to guide them back to love and light. As a newly trained alchemist, it is your job to now practice compassion for the folks spinning their wheels in self-doubt. It is your time to be a shining example of what is available in transformation. This doesn't mean we turn transformation into a new religion where we have it right and others are doing it wrong. It is your turn to display the benefits of establishing your own core values, sense of self, and doing the work of introspection. It is your job to model alignment and all the freedom that comes with it.

As you do this, you will experience yourself as that unique expression of love in the world. You will witness your own maturity blossoming in the moment. You will be modeling what you are teaching them and they will not only hear what you are saying, they will get to experience it at the same time, through your example.

I will never forget the time a client told me, "I practiced listening to my husband the way you listen to me and it caused one of the best conversations we've ever had. I listened without judgment and didn't add anything to what he said. I reflected what I heard and it kept us in a constructive conversation that helped us reach a new level of our relationship."

My big, coachy heart was bursting with every word. I felt astonished about the subtle, yet powerful ripple effect of this work.

Who you are makes a massive difference in this world. How you are in this world contributes to the Cycle of Hurt or Love at all times. Constantly check in about which you prefer to be in alignment with. Constantly realign with your cell role and show up for it, fully. You are so important. It is time you get to experience and appreciate your authentic impact as much as everyone else does. Keep being the gift that you are by choosing it more intentionally, and don't forget to have a *lot* of fun while you're at it.

Chapter 13

Only the Highest Good

I have been mentioning 'the highest good of all' frequently throughout this book, and it is time to shine a spotlight on this concept. This is the Alignment Pillar. This is about being in impeccable alignment with what serves the Collective, and I don't just mean humanity. This includes Momma Earth, the plants and animals, the atmosphere and sky, the stars and galaxies, and everything in between. This is relevant on a physical and energetic level.

Physically, we must take responsibility for sharing this planet. We have a massive Impact, individually and collectively. As a species, we have been generally reckless about our use of resources, and many generations haven't considered the planet that their lineage will inherit. The wellbeing of the planet and all its inhabitants has been put in danger as a result of the negative environmental impact of each generation, combined with an increasing population. Consciousness in this area has only become important in the last few decades.

I bring this up because it is pretty clear that each generation born is a more evolved generation. This seems like quite the opposite of what we hear in living rooms at family parties when Great-Auntie Janis starts story-telling about, 'back in my day…'" However, each generation born comes to Earth and raises the frequency of humanity in their own right. When zoomed into a micro level, it seems easy to criticize a generation. When zoomed out, it is clear the ways a generation has innovated and straight-up trail blazed new paths from the point that the last generation stopped. This is moving us down the path of total enlightenment.

I like to think of each human life as a brick in the road of the evolution of humanity. We all come here to be a contribution. The extent to which we fulfill that role or not is to be determined on an individual basis. We all came to lay our brick in the road, but if we are not actively aligning ourselves with the highest good of all, or 'HGA,' we could be laying our brick on a road that takes us off the path of Collective enlightenment.

When I think of my own brick, I think of my company Hearts Unleashed. I know that I will be, do, and have a lot of things in this lifetime, and that my biggest contribution will be my willingness to allow infinite intelligence to move to and through me with as little ego interference as possible. This has allowed me to write my books, record my podcasts, coach and guide other leaders, and more. Blocking ego interference is challenging and a lifelong process if you are committed to alignment, but it is necessary. It is also always worth it.

I take a lot of pride in Hearts Unleashed and feel confident saying that we have made a massive impact with our work of translating transformation for the Collective. We are committed to unleashing the true and authentic hearts of all, which also contributes to our species' shift. We all need to be operating with emotional intelligence so that we are consciously contributing to our cooperation and collaboration. It is a contribution to humanity to align with HGA.

What I know about the work that I have done is that it is for the highest good of all. My work impacts individuals and groups directly, and that is fun to witness on a day-to-day basis, but the ripple effect is incomprehensible. I love to share that I cannot clothe all the naked. I cannot feed all the hungry. I cannot shelter all the homeless, but what I can do is unleash every heart that I encounter knowing that their passions will be unleashed to begin transforming parts of this world that my two hands, two eyes, one mouth, and one heart cannot possibly do alone. Each of us subscribing to a more harmonious coexistence is what will bring it about.

We are not meant to do this alone. We are meant to practice interdependence and serve each other with our unique gifts as to contribute to the highest good of all. Using HGA as a reference for yourself in your decision-making process is the perfect tool and opportunity to practice and gauge mastery level alignment. The simple question that I shared in the last chapter "is this in alignment?" will clear your path quickly if you are committed to using it like a compass on a hike. It will always lead you home.

Another thing that will always lead you home is your intuition. I often refer to it as 'my spidey senses.' When I get a ping, zing, or nudge from my intuition, I work to always honor it and it always leads me toward the highest good of all. Be gentle with yourself my friend, this is a learned skill and we all miss a beat every once in a while. It is more about the commitment to staying on track that will keep you on track. Your ego will want you to do your own things for your sole benefit and some-times at the cost of others. Your ego's infatuation with staying safe, comfortable, and looking good will side-track you sometimes, and that's okay. This occurrence is natural, and you can progress through it by realigning with the highest good as frequently as necessary.

As I mentioned in the last chapter, the HGA is always in your best interest. Keep in mind that your fullest life is far greater than your limited brain could ever dream of. Your ego won't believe that, and you will attempt to force outcomes and manipulate the process to your own accord. This just sets you up for difficulty, complications, and a generally empty feeling inside. When we compromise our integrity for shortcuts to power, material wealth, or success, we will know it. Our intuition will get louder and more obvious to signal the detour we have taken off the path of enlightenment. We often experience discomfort in our physical bodies that is caused by our energetic body's attempt to com-municate with us, to tell us that we have gone astray from the HGA and direct us back to center. This is a great and powerful internal guidance system and if we would surrender to it, we would be living greater and longer lives while still being a contribution. Whenever you are struggling with hearing and following your intuition, remind yourself that your Higher Power has more in store for you than you could ever imagine. Your personal task is about learning to listen, align, trust, allow, and receive.

Your intuition will guide you in this. It will send signals as thoughts, feelings, and body sensations to get your attention. This can be tricky, because your ego does this too. If you are feeling some type of internal battle, it is because you are having a hard time identifying which version of you is speaking up. Do not fret, my friend. There is a way to know the difference.

The heart whispers and the brain screams. The soul speaks and the ego shouts. If you are hearing worried thoughts and chatter, that is not you at your highest and best, which means there will not be any guidance or answers coming from that voice. This is the voice of fear, and you will know this if you pay close attention to how that voice makes you feel. You will likely feel crumby, anxious, sad, angry, shameful, or any other form of judgment you naturally suffer from. On the other hand, intuition has a very powerful and resounding depth to its statements. You can feel a wave of truth rush over you when you clearly receive a message from spirit. These feel better to the body. These messages may feel bold as well; bolder than you currently are to follow through with them, but they are true nonetheless. Those are the messages to trust.

You were born authentic and bold, babe. As a baby, you cried when you had a need. You pooped and let someone else clean it up. You burped and farted without embarrassment and more. Little baby you laughed loudly and played hard. Then as people started to correct you, you started to correct yourself. This is when you became confused about the voices in your head. The ego voice, or inner critic, is a collection of all the critical voices you have listened to over the years. This collective voice is made up of parents, family, friends, teachers, coaches, authority figures, all the way up to religion, school, and society. There are some loud statements made by these factors and you adopt many of them as your own, when likely, they are not. To understand this and begin to disassociate from this voice will free you up to step into alignment with your intuition.

Trusting the communications of the soul takes courage as well. In reference to alignment, being able to ask 'is this in alignment?" *and* to actually honor the answer you hear from deep within is the real alignment. We hear our guidance all the time and ignore it. We see red flags in relationships and justify them. We know we aren't happy in our work or environment and stay anyways. We hear a perfectly clear instruction about our health and keep smoking, drinking, and eating. We see all the signs we ask for from the Universe and look the other way or pretend to be distracted.

I like to consider this selective blindness. We selectively overlook things that make us uncomfortable so that we don't have to be uncomfortably bold. Unfortunately, this puts us out of alignment and even out of integrity in many areas of life. As a result of the avoidance, things start to pile up and unravel. We start to have anxiety and slip right into judgment, flinging it in every direction.

My guess is that if you believed you had a choice in the matter, you wouldn't want to be and live that way. If you think about the pillars of this book, with two of three knocked out, you would certainly not feel like you are winning the game of life. I choose to believe that you would rather feel authentically great and that shortcuts won't cut it for you anymore. For the sake of your highest and best, it is your duty to always align yourself with HGA, and then get to work on the integrity it takes to choose it again and again.

I say it takes integrity because failure to be courageous and boldly authentic has a lot to do with unresolved trauma, incompletion, and projection. If you have fear about following the guidance of your intuition, it is likely that somewhere along the line, you collected evidence that it is unsafe to be your authentic, bold self. If you find this to be true, reference the Integrity Pillar to clean up the messy areas in your life preventing you from getting into alignment, because if you practice the due diligence of integrity, you will pretty naturally evolve into alignment.

Alignment in this way will create more alignment.

It feels good to be in alignment and it feels good to feel good. The biggest challenge of this is the training that leads to consistent awareness and more automatic recalibration. Once you've got it, you get clear about how valuable it is. When you are experiencing alignment frequently, anything else becomes naturally intolerable and your ability to detect being out of whack becomes elevated. Over time, it simply becomes second nature to stop compromising your integrity and alignment.

The realest skill of alignment is being able to tap into your intuition at a moment's notice and use it as the compass in your minute-to-minute existence. This skill is about sharpening the senses by releasing any and all habits, patterns, and addictions of the body and mind that can cloud your discernment. What that might mean is that you finally quit smoking, leave that toxic relationship, or quit harming yourself in the million ways we humans do. Again, requires your boldness, because although disempowering patterns are widely accepted, they are not in alignment with the highest good of all.

It is one thing to know what to do. It is an entirely other thing to do it. What stops us from utilizing our internal guidance systems is the lifelong conditioning to doubt our inner authority. You hear your body talking to you and you ignore it; one, out of personal craving, and two, out of conditioning to take the easy route. When partying is normalized and sex is glamorized, it is hard to say no for the mentally and emotionally underdeveloped individual. Prioritizing alignment will come after exhausting a lifestyle that depletes you. You will know very clearly from within that it is time to shed addictions that no longer serve you. Then, there will come a very important point in your life when you return to your most true nature, and from that point, nothing can stop you from reaching your highest and best.

This is when we get to fully explore the concept of the integrity rampage! *Yaaaaayyyy!* I have been eagerly awaiting our arrival to this point because it is one of my favorite aspects of evolution and it is often the most memorable as well. It is my favorite ritual of transformation to suddenly become serious about cleaning up the areas of your life that are out of order.

I briefly explained this in the Integrity Pillar because duh, integrity, but this is really an application of alignment. Over the course of your graduation from self discovery, to development, to mastery, it will become crystal clear what no longer serves you. At different stages, this awareness will hit new levels of intolerable.

My most dramatic integrity rampage was a year after my divorce, when I discovered that I was quite a pack rat, hoarding memorabilia as proof of a life once lived. At that time, I had a deep subconscious belief that your value was based on the sum of your life, so I was sure to have proof of my value on display in picture frames, trophies, trinkets, and collections. The exact instant that I realized my value exists solely within, my apartment suddenly felt like the most extreme hoarding situation ever. In reality, I was clean, tidy, and organized, but I had so much physical stuff that it suddenly felt claustrophobic.

Over the next month, I sold, donated, tossed out, and burned about seventy percent of my possessions. When it was all said and done, I felt like I had lost a hundred pounds of emotional weight. It was crazy how new I felt. I felt restored and lighter. I felt free.

I felt so free that I packed what fit in my Jeep and moved to California the next month. With all of that stuff gone, my mind and heart reached complete clarity about my next aligned step to take in life. I had always wanted to live in California, but as long as I held onto all the evidence of who I had been, I wasn't free to become anyone else. Shedding and releasing my past freed me up to head into my future, boldly.

I have integrity rampages frequently, but I want to teach you a lesson that will save you tons of time, effort, and energy. This lesson is in alignment with my *8 Pillars of Empowerment* methodology in my self mastery course, called *UNLEASHED*. Knowing the eight pillars will allow you to actively choose to live an empowered life consistently, without having to constantly upturn it in the name of transformation. For more information and access to the digital course, visit abigailgazda.com/unleashed.

I would like to teach the lesson of integrity rampages with an analogy: transformation is like an earthquake. First, there is the unexpected quake, aka your awakening. It comes unannounced, is an unexpected shock, and shakes up everything, destroying a lot. From here, there are some aftermath tremors, or more new awarenesses, that dismantle more areas of life. There is a lot of irreversible damage, as well as a lot to process at first. This is the beginning of transformation: Awakening and Awareness.

The next part of the process is Acknowledgement and Acceptance. You must acknowledge the damage done and accept it, in order to effectively begin the recovery process. In terms of an earthquake, this starts with the general cleanup of debris. From there, you assess the damage and evaluate your next steps. If your house is deemed inhabitable, the next step is to start demolishing and deconstructing. Let's say the whole house must come down, then the next step is to prepare the land to rebuild. The ground must be graded and restored to support a new foundation, and that foundation must be laid.

This is where the next two stages of transformation come in: Application and Accountability. Before this earthquake, you had built your house on a shaky foundation. This is why when a natural disaster struck, your whole house came crumbling down. It wasn't strong enough to begin with. Applying the lessons of the last house, along with hiring professionals to help you rebuild with integrity will make this next one strong and beautiful. Something you will look forward to living in.

The last two stages are ones that reflect putting the finishing touches on your beautiful, new home. This is where you have reached Self Mastery and Transcendence in your transformation. What is left to do in this house is hang curtains, polish surfaces, and pick out paint colors. There is a lot less upheaval in the transformational work, and you get to enjoy the fruits of your labor.

Best yet, you have turned a tragedy into a triumph. The stages of transformation here are Activation and Activated Action. When we first experience this earthquake, we go all in on the project to get it to the point of having a beautiful new home. The process starts out rough and continuously gets easier, simpler, and even more enjoyable.

Red alert, this point is so important that I feel inclined to repeat it: the process of transformation starts out rough and continuously gets *easier, simpler, and even more enjoyable.*

Do not unconsciously make it hard on yourself as time goes on. Your first few integrity rampages will involve a lot of upheaval. There was the time that I got rid of seventy percent of my possessions. There was the time I left my full-time job to launch my coaching practice. There was the time I completely cleared my schedule and stopped letting other people put things on there without my permission. These were times of disruption, demolition, and dismantling. I wish I wore a hard hat in those days 'cause damn, life was heavily under construction at that time.

The good news is it doesn't stay crazy. When you start to shift, your integrity rampages become less extreme as well. This is a great thing, so let it be. We become so accustomed to the upheaval that we cause more problems than we solve. Pump the breaks on that and realize that integrity in the stages of self mastery and transcendence is not as extreme.

This is the point of running through your life with a fine-tooth comb. Some of my own examples looked like no longer accepting client calls on weekends or before 10a.m. and having three-day weekends. It looked like getting a bookkeeper and making a plan to get out of debt. It looked like moving from Arizona to California because I knew that was where my soul wanted to be. It looked like giving up alcohol, cannabis, coffee, and sugar. It looked like stopping mental addictions like worry, doubt, blame, drama, and anxiety. It looked like cleaning out my closet twice a year. These didn't require whole lifestyle shifts. At the points of these integrity shifts, I just became more elevated by each and every adjustment.

Integrity is really about alignment, because it is about following through on what is good and right for the soul. One must know themselves well to be in alignment. You cannot be in alignment if you are not clear about what you are aligning with. That is why in the last chapter, I gave you the concept of core values and a sense of self to anchor into. In the next part of this book, I will provide you with the utmost important anchor; faith.

Aligning your life with faith will be your North Star in every aspect of your life and decision you make. Integrity will be about the minor details that lift you above your humanness, up out of the 3D, and closer to your divine Source Energy. This shift is the greatest gift, because you are liberated to unleash your heart and soul onto the world, and it actually feels exhilarating.

At these levels, your leadership and mission feels like second nature, and the only lifestyle you would ever want to live. Your Higher Power and Spirit rejoices to have another human laying a brick in the direction of enlightenment and conspires to flood you with the abundance necessary to help you along your path. This is where co-creation becomes natural, fluid, and fun. This is where the truest identity of your soul will begin to reveal itself, and you will start permitting yourself to embody your own inner authority, fully. The world will get to witness it, too.

I look forward to witnessing you in all of your glory.

Chapter 14

Power Tools of Transformation

Ok, my friend. As we begin to wrap up this Alignment Pillar, I want to provide you with a handful of power tools to add to your toolbox of transformation. I am going to rattle off some methods for awareness, and how you can use them in your daily life to keep yourself empowered along your path.

As an energetic being, you are a sponge. As a human being, you are quite literally a sponge. In both senses, you absorb the world around you. You take on others energy and emotions. You take in pollution from the air. You pick up the light and darkness of others. You drink up moisture and pick up germs. We are naturally spongy, folks.

This is not the worst problem to have, but it can really mess with you if you are not aware or intentional about this truth. As a sponge, you are constantly being wrung out, as well. Some people prefer to use the 'you can't serve from an empty cup' adage and while that is true, I think it is too overused to have the same impact. People's automatic response to the empty cup is "ahhh, yeah yeah, I know. I just don't….*insert b.s. excuses*…"

As a sponge, you are walking around your entire day absorbing everything around you and then other spongy folk walk up and soak up some of your energy. If all day long, people are wringing you dry and you are out there soaking up coffee, gasoline, and bacon grease, eventually you are going to start running on fumes, or be malnourished. I am having a lot of fun with this analogy, but it can become a real problem when we are not taking great care of ourselves on a daily basis.

It is completely and utterly your responsibility for how you show up and what you get out of the world. I spent most of the Integrity Pillar talking about that idea, so I'll refer you back to it to keep clearing and accepting your responsibility, in order to make the most of this life. What I want to make clear in this chapter is that when you are out in the world, you can make the choice about what you absorb.

To be at a personal peak performance level and showing up for an extraordinary life, you will need to know a few things about how to protect yourself, to stay in integrity, alignment, and faith. These skills are *still* meant to help you show up as a leader in life, not walk around the world protecting yourself from social and environmental dangers. This is about transcending humanness so that you are impenetrable, while also being positively impactful.

This is a chapter to practice discernment. By being

spongy and taking on a lot, we must become more aware of what we are taking on. Similarly, we must educate and empower ourselves to not take on what doesn't serve us. We generally live in an obnoxiously loud and busy world. In this Information Age, we have things beeping at us, people talking loudly, and lots of influences flying at us from every angle. It can get pretty intense.

If you are not clear and sure about yourself, it can cause you to shrink to avoid it, and this can be detrimental to your unleashing. This can also quickly deteriorate your 'emotional endurance' or 'emotional immunity.' These ideas work exactly like athleticism or health. Having great stamina empowers one to run far and for long periods of time. Great health keeps you upbeat, active, and alert. Both contribute to wellbeing and longevity. If you meet someone who fits this description, you can probably count on meeting them with a smile on their face and a light in their eyes.

On the other hand, unfit, unhealthy people are usually low energy, low vibe, and struggling with something. They likely lean toward pessimism and deal with exhaustion. Usually, they are pretty exhausting to be around, because their sponge is saturated with gunk and they are looking for a shot of something to feel better. They have no endurance, stamina, or vitality. Life seems to be a drag for these folks. Bless them. We can all probably think of a few and it doesn't make them any less of a person. This may have been you at one point or another. It may be how you are feeling now. Either way, we are alchemizing judgment and practicing being understanding of all frequency levels.

I want to teach you about emotional endurance and immunity because when you are in tip-top physical shape, you don't tire climbing up the stairs. If you have a great health regimen, illness doesn't exactly take you out. If you have emotional endurance, holding a vision of a long-term goal won't tire you out before attaining it. If you have a strong emotional immune system, negative feedback won't send you into a spiral of self-doubt.

This is everything when it comes to alignment, because there are infinite factors that can get in your way, slow you down, or stop you from staying committed to your highest and best. I like to keep the concept of emotional endurance and immunity as simple as it is. The same rules of health and wellbeing of the body apply to the health and wellbeing of the heart, mind, and soul.

- Adequate sleep
- Allow appropriate rest and rejuvenation
- Hydration
- Proper nutrition
- Positive activity, learning, and appropriate challenges
- Restorative activities
- Healthy hobbies
- Spiritual practices such as journaling, mediation, and prayer
- Empowering relationships
- Introspection and personal development practices

There may be a few more that suit you more personally but I want to display how simple it is to stay empowered in your life. If all of these are not a part of your daily, or at the very least, weekly routine, you are denying yourself your own health and wellness. It is that straight forward and there are really no excuses about why you cannot incorporate these. If you are blessed enough to afford this book and be reading it, I am certain you have the resources and options to make your life a powerful one.

I have spent a lot of this book highlighting patterns, habits, and behaviors that disempower us, so I am not going to use this chapter to share what they are. What I would like to do is share a distinction for you to check in with yourself when you are faced with a decision that may take you out of alignment. When something unexpected flies up in your face, before absorbing it, ask yourself, "is this an invitation or a temptation?" Consider an invitation something positive and empowering and a temptation the opposite. Our ego loves to tempt us to slip back into our old ways and make a mess in our lives. You will always have opportunities to slip up and that is why you must be able to recognize temptation coming a mile down the track. In the beginning of transformation, we may have already fallen for temptation before we snap out of its trance and realize we've slipped. This is okay.

In terms of emotional endurance, the goal is to be able to run farther and longer without slipping up or slowing down. This happens through training. In terms of immunity, this is about being immune to temptation.

It cannot take you over and make you sick. This is where your decision-making power will save you time and time again. Alignment plays its most important role with temptation because it requires recognition and a conscious choice to stay in alignment with HGA.

This also works with invitations. As you grow, so will your opportunities. This will also require you to practice discernment, because saying yes to every opportunity would wring you dry and leave you exhausted, confused, and disheartened. This is just another skill to master. The best part is this is not too difficult when you are clear about your commitments. The real challenge of this phase and skill is becoming more comfortable and masterful at saying no and declining offers in an empowered way.

This is a great time to stop using "I'm too busy" as an excuse or reason for not doing something. If you are empowered and at choice about your life, then you are at choice about your schedule, even if it is planned by the hour every week. That is not busy. That is aligned with what you have prioritized. That means that when someone offers you something out of alignment with your life and commitments, you could practice something like, "thank you for the offer/invitation, my schedule is already full of fun and exciting things that I am working on and committed to!"

What a different answer, right? People even appreciate that level of honesty because they can sense you really considered their offer and can understand that you actively declined, which ultimately moves the opportunity to the next right prospect. Glee! Look at you contributing to the HGA! You old pro, you.

The last tool I would like to share with your spongy self is the concept of shielding. This is immensely valuable and has helped me daily since I learned it many moons ago. Because there are so many influential factors out in the world and their wavelengths are constantly swirling around you, I want you to imagine that you have a protective bubble around you. This invisible forcefield is, as always, meant for you to do this work in the world, not separate you from others.

As we go about our day-to-day lives, I have shared how many people are irresponsible about their impact. They are running around their day spewing shit all over others because they are not doing their own inner work. While their inner work is not your responsibility, being an example of love, peace, light, acceptance, and joy is. If you absorb someone else's stuff and do not know how to effectively alchemize it quickly, it can take you out too and have you both out there recklessly contributing to the Cycle of Hurt.

So to play it safe, I want to empower you to use shielding when necessary. You simply imagine this invisible orb around your body that darkness cannot penetrate. Judgment cannot make its way through to you. This is a valuable tool while learning alchemy, because like endurance, you must be able to run three miles straight before you can run six miles without stopping. Some people have darker, more aggressive energy than a developing alchemist is prepared for, and that's okay.

What your new shield helps you do is actually stand in a situation, safely observing someone spewing or lashing out, without it impacting you negatively. This is a fascinating experience, much like watching a scene in slow motion. You are able to witness someone's anger without making it about you and that gives you a chance to see that person's pain. It helps you shift out of reaction and into compassion.

This is where we get to start bringing the magic and mysticism back into this work because your heart will start transmuting what you are witnessing back into love. Granted, this may not happen overnight, but the more you shield and witness, the more familiar you will become with seeing the source of others' pain. When you don't listen from your own filters, you can suddenly hear the messages they are actually communicating without them saying out loud:

- I'm scared
- I'm lonely
- I'm hurt
- I feel misunderstood
- No one is listening to me (and I have something to say)
- I feel unheard/unseen
- I feel worthless/unworthy
- I hate myself
- I don't feel safe
- I can't trust anyone or myself
- And the list goes on and on...

My dear, I hope your heart feels as wide open as

mine does right now, because I know that you know we are all good at our core. One of my favorite reminders of this is that even Lucifer was a fallen angel. Our darkness, meanness, or nastiness is an indication of how disconnected we are from our Source Energy. It displays how separate we are and feel.

I am well aware of some of the most terrible, incomprehensible atrocities that humans can manage to do to one another, but life has done that to us. We were born pure. We were born with that golden umbilical and some of us never found the thread in our later years. It is an unfortunate occurrence and if you are committed to being an alchemist, you are committed to opening up your heart to all. I am clear about the level of love required for that and it may take time. I am simply making the invitation to arrive there when you feel ready, willing, and able.

When it comes to shielding, we have the opportunity to love the ones who seem the toughest, because what there is to know is that we do not need to change or fix anyone on this planet. We need to love ourselves so fully that we allow our own light to shine. The coolest part about shielding is that although darkness cannot come in, your light can certainly shine out.

As an alchemist in training, this gives you the opportunity to witness others' pain, yes. It also grants you front row access to watch the result of you radiating in this world. Keep shining, my dear. The world needs more light.

Chapter 15

Clarity

Would ya look at that, we have arrived at the end of the Alignment Pillar; clarity! Are you feeling clear, my dear? Let's review this pillar to really check in on your current state of alignment.

Alignment is where integrity and faith intersect. This part of the book has provided clear detail about how you, as the human you are, can make the connection between these two pillars. You are a conduit for love energy making the leap from the fifth dimension and landing right on your heart here in the 3D. Being a clear channel for that love energy to leap is what brings into form on the planet and makes your life rich with abundance.

Clarity is alignment in full operation. Clarity is what leads to transcendence, which I will discuss fully in the upcoming Faith Pillar. Clarity establishes a certainty within us that supports our alignment, empowerment, and enlightenment. People with clarity are operating at full capacity or are at least in the process of arriving at that level of wholeness.

If we take a look back at the various aspects of this pillar as a checklist, we can more quickly identify where we are out of alignment when we are feeling funky on any given day.

- Understanding frequencies and accessing the different dimensions
- Connecting with our Source Energy and Higher Power frequently
- Knowing and re-presencing your core values
- Maintaining and evolving your sense of self
- Knowing and accepting your role as a cell in the body of humanity
- Having clarity of commitments
- Blessing and releasing anything not for the HGA
- Activating integrity rampages
- Utilizing the 8 Pillars of Empowerment Methodology to stay empowered
- Protecting, sourcing, and shielding your energy
- Honoring yourself as a developing alchemist
- Practicing the commitment of accepting and loving all beings and things
- Hearing and honoring your guidance as a vehicle for abundance and love

What a powerful checklist, eh? Internalizing this checklist as a personal commitment to being your highest and best will train you so well as an alchemist, that I promise there will be a day that you no longer need to reference it. That being said, it's always good to review it once a year, even if just to reminisce on your times of growth and development. Functioning by this list will have you in full alignment, and as soon as we add the information packed into the Faith Pillar, you are going to be a beaming, radiant being, whose light could guide the darkest souls home.

I've saved one of the bullet points on that list for this chapter, because I want it to be the last point I make about alignment before moving into the faith conversation: clarity of commitments. On the most basic, human level, each of our souls took a body to fulfill these baseline commitments on planet Earth:

- To love and be loved
- To be a contribution
- To serve
- To evolve
- To guide
- To experience this 3D reality to our fullest potential

If each and every human were to be fully honest with themselves, they could sense these basic human commitments within. If we cannot identify them, we are not fully tapped into our soul and source. This simply takes more deconditioning of the humanness that blocks this awareness, as well as personal discovery and development of the soul self.

We all came here to fulfill these commitments on different scales and capacities and yet, there is room for all of us to do so. In fact, consider how well we would be functioning interdependently if everyone were honoring these basic human commitments. Abundance in its truest nature would be blossoming, and humanity would be thriving. We would find and create functional means of coexistence that serve the highest good of all, and *that* is what we are striving to arrive at.

Now that you are clear about the commitments of your soul, you may align yourself with all that feels good and right and experience the fullest version of yourself and your life. It is by the function of your internal guidance system that you will have the pleasure of adding your unique flavors to the recipe of these basic human commitments. We all show up for them. How we show up for them is what makes us unique, divine, and important.

My friend, my loving request is that you use all of the content, information, and tools in this book to lay your brick in the road of humanity, in the direction that leads us back to the Garden State.

Share this knowledge, it is not exclusive. Share this wisdom. It belongs to each of us. Connect people back to The Source. It is home for every one of us, and we all deserve to feel at home.

Faith Pillar

Chapter 16

Trust & Transcendence

We have arrived at the third and final pillar; faith. My ego has slowed me down many times to prevent me getting to this point, yet here we are, together. I am telling myself that if I haven't lost you by now, I must put my own fear aside and trust that you are ready, willing, and open to receive what I have to share in this pillar. I am currently exercising faith, in order to teach it.

I am practicing faith that what I say is true on the fundamental level, and that hearts around the world will be open enough to consider these truths as an expression of their own. I am surrendering my fears and insecurities to let my fingers scurry along this keyboard to get this message out. I am releasing my concern about this message of faith being adequate, 'correct' to others' 3D spiritual beliefs, and respectful of each person's (non)religious background.

I have never before had the level of faith it takes to write this book. Over the past few years, I have been guided through personal and spiritual initiations of divine intervention that have prepared my heart to know God. Prior, I had actively resisted a relationship with the God Consciousness, ever since Catholic grade school. I share in my first book, *Giving Up Giving Up: The Memoir of a Quitter*, how I slowly quit religion because religion felt more like an academic class than a belief system.

I share in that book that I never actually felt connected to God for myself, and therefore, had never internalized a relationship with him that caused me to show up to church on Sundays. It was always an association of obligation, and since I rejected the faith, I rejected the center of that faith: God.

The way that religion was associated with school made it just a grade in my eyes; learn the parables, memorize the 'characters,' remember the dates/locations, regurgitate the lessons, and get the grade. There was nothing authentic or energizing about it for me. There was nothing organic about it, nor did it make me feel connected to a force greater than myself. In fact, if I had any faith at all at the time, it was believing that my Grammy Rose was my Guardian Angel, looking out for me from the clouds, preventing me from making mistakes and wrecking my car. I would hardly call that a spiritual connection, but it was all I had in my times of confusion and rejection of faith.

This began to shift after my personal awakening of divorce. It certainly didn't happen right away; rather, it has been a four year long unfolding that has led to this exact moment of feeling empowered to teach you what

I know. In the very beginning of this book, I shared with you that the source of all that is, is Love. Love is the core of everything. We all have direct access to it because we come directly from it, and we go back directly to it. So, if you are anything like me four years ago, know that when I reference God, I am referencing unwavering, unconditional, unaltered Love as an entity itself. I am actively choosing to use the name God because of how confronting it was for me to work through.

So many people have been hurt, harmed, and ridiculed in the name of God and recreating my understanding of the God expression of Love has been the most challenging for me. I have felt called to share the benevolence of God so that it may bring even one human closer to the love available in the healing of what we might call 'the God wound.' Our relationship with this entity has not really been our own. It has been so heavily influenced by other human beings, who may also not have an understanding of the true nature of God.

As I shared about past generations not having the same support we do to heal and thrive, our elders have not had all the best examples of their own spiritual connection. Humanity as a whole has been largely separated from its spiritual nature. We have hardly had our own interpretation of God. We have not been taught to have a connection with God, we have been taught what to think, how to think, how to act, and how not to act. These rules weren't established by God, they were created by man in the name of God. I am inviting you into your own, new union with God.

A few years back, it dawned on me; Muslims believe that Allah loves them, Hindus believe that Krishna loves them, Buddhists believe that Buddha loves them. Sikhs, Christians, Catholics, and Jews all believe that God loves them. If we all want to believe in one universal truth, it is that we are loved. We are willing to practice incredible amounts of faith that we inherently deserve love from a source, and we do not have to 'earn' it. In this dimension, we humans have had a lot of difficulty collectively mastering the unconditional level of love that we count on from our Higher Powers. What I realized during this discovery is that anyone can name their Higher Power anything. We are all talking about, trusting in, and praying to a source of unconditional Love.

To be really specific, even 'Love' is also just another word for it. At the core of all that exists, there are no words. There is no definition. It is out beyond the fifth dimension that any and all separation completely disappears. In order to help explain it, we must define it and shape it for comprehension, but the more you come to know it for yourself, the more you understand there really are no words for it. When you know this, you also know it doesn't matter what you call it. It is all that is. It is the truth and the light. It is everything and it is nothing. You just know or you don't. It is my commitment in this pillar that you gain access to it.

So while I will reference God in this Pillar most frequently, you are welcome to swap out your favorite 3D, human-mind-constructed representation of Love. I will be using his holy name because it has caused me the most turmoil and growth over the course of my life and if I can help even one heart heal their relationship with him, I will have done the job I hoped to do.

I will never forget how pissed off I was in my coach training program during the month we covered spirituality for our training. "Why does this have to be about 'God!?!'" I scowled. I actually skipped some of the journaling prompts that asked directly about God and jumped to the ones about spirituality because I did not relate to them as one in the same. I could tell the leaders were producing their desired results of triggering us with the use of 'God' and it pissed me off even more. It was proving some point that I didn't even know it was proving, and I could not recognize the lesson at the time. Instead, I struggled most of my way through that month and held my breath until it was over.

This training situation didn't bring me any closer to God at the time, but it certainly revealed some serious completion work I wasn't aware of needing. I thought that because I was vaguely spiritual and believed in my Grammy Rose Guardian Angel that I was doing okay in the spiritual realm. It had not seemed important to heal my broken relationship with God. I believed that so fully that I worked on integrity and alignment in every other area of my entire life before arriving to the conclusion that the necessity of healing my relationship with God was never going to fade away.

You guys, when I say every other area, I mean it. Relationships, health, career, wellbeing, relocation, past traumas, business, finances, current events, world issues, others' transformations, underwater basket weaving, you name it. I did every single thing possible to get away with just never having a relationship with God. I started more spirituality practices like meditation, journaling, and channeling to feel like it was enough. The more integrous and aligned I became everywhere else in life, the more obvious it became that God wanted to make a connection. What I knew about my behavior is that the way I was now avoiding it meant it was going to be the most important breakthrough I could have to access my next level self, life, and purpose.

It took the most incredible human being I know, my husband Timothy, to bring me home to God. Also a coach, he has a coaching ministry that serves from its own unique commitment to help any and all that are willing to come closer to God. To my heart, Timothy is an Earth Angel with a direct line to God and has helped me shed my lifelong grudges against the idea of God as well as get many of my personal questions answered.

I had a pretty decent personal-development-style spirituality practice of journaling and meditating when I met Timothy, and he kept inviting me to pray. I remember ignoring his first few invitations as if I hadn't heard them. Fortunately for me, he didn't stop encouraging and also didn't stop asking if I had prayed about whatever I was lamenting about. "Eh, I wrote about it but I didn't pray about it," I would often answer, kind of timidly. I was really putting off his prayer strategy as if it were a strategy. I didn't believe in who I thought I was praying to, so it felt pointless and even frustrating.

It was after a bit more avoiding that he shifted his invitation from praying to God to exploring who I thought God was. "What I know to be true about God is that he is omnipotent and benevolent," he would gently offer. Now, bless this brilliant man because he uses many words that aren't in my vocabulary and keeps me learning. When I looked up those two words, just to be sure, I remembered that age-old chant from grade school "God is good, all the time! All the time, God is good!" This brought an innocent memory and smile back to my face, and I became more open to what he had to say.

Over months, he kept sharing with me exactly how omnipotent and benevolent God is by reminding me daily with the same patience, grace, poise, and certainty. He didn't so much tell me as he did show me through his own display of inner peace. He listened to my judgment and resistance without judgment or resistance.

Things really shifted when Timothy helped me see that my understanding of God is not my own. My visual of God was based on the Catholic version, gray-haired man in the sky who greets you with a scroll of your sins upon your arrival at the pearly gates. He sits there waiting for you on your judgment day, like…really? "Judgment Day?" ready to review your life and make the deciding factor on your eternity. This was the idea of God that I resisted and rejected.

Beyond my intimidating imagery, I had a bone to pick with Mr. God: Why did my parents have to get divorced? Why did my mom struggle? Why did my dad struggle? Why do bad things happen to good people? Why do people do horrific things to each other? Why is there hunger, illness, and suffering? Why, why, why?

Most of us have our particular flavor of this barrage of unanswered questions for God and many of us never get our answers. Instead, we keep our resentment for a universal identity that has become the scapegoat of our Earthly turmoil. I had a lot of grudges, resentments, and resignations about him as a being, and had collected enough evidence against him to not feel safe trusting him with my life and prosperity. I didn't really feel like relying on him to come through for me after feeling so on my own throughout life.

From divorced parents, to tearing my ACL in college basketball, to the disappointment of my teaching career being nothing I expected, to divorce, to the pain of divorce, I just didn't really believe that God was all that great. From my own life to witnessing incredible struggles in others' lives, I couldn't sense the presence of God. He felt pretty made-up to me, and that made me angry because it felt like a means of man-made control and power. In a world that has so much pain and suffering on massive and criminal scales, I could not comprehend how this God we were all praying to wasn't interjecting to bring justice, protection, and peace to our world.

I was in full-fledged doubt of this omnipotent and benevolent God. Sprinkle in the Catholic Guilt concepts about the wrath of God and the expectation of being 'God-fearing' people and it was a 'hell no' to the whole idea of God. I was pretty closed off to relating to him as a source that could be trusted or relied on. I was deeply resistant to putting my trust in a 'man' I had not 'met' but was somehow expected to count on.

I have never been more vulnerable about my complete and utter distrust of this entity until right now. Naturally, I have kept it mostly to myself for fear of offending. I was afraid of turning away readers of great faith in God, but I want to be real about the actual evolution I have had. I know that I am not alone and while you may have not had my exact experience, I am guessing you can relate in a few ways. Although it feels vulnerable, it feels well worth sharing because if I can heal my relationship with him, there could be something available for you to learn, too. Again, this doesn't have to be about G-O-D. It may simply be about connecting to a source greater than you. Here on this plane, even connecting with the breath and life of nature is a force greater than you. Whatever or whoever your Higher Power is, I can tell you that it will become important somewhere down the line if you are truly committed to HGA. Being connected to The Source is the only way to access the HGA.

It was in a conversation with Timothy when my whole barrier blocking God's infinite love came crumbling down. I was going on and on about all of my valid justifications for not counting on God and he reflected to me that I was not talking about my relationship with God, but actually, my relationship with men on this planet. Mind blown.

Immediately, everything shifted. I let that wall come down with a deep exhale and drop of my shoulders. Decades of emotional weight slid off my back and I felt held; not by Timothy at the moment, by God himself. All that time, Timothy had reminded me that he was omnipotent and benevolent. Upon my individual acceptance of that truth, I felt lifted up in a hug of homecoming celebration. Love never goes away. It just patiently waits for your permission to bless you. God waits ever so patiently to wrap you up in his love, abundance, grace, and guidance.

Immediately following that breakthrough, I came back down to Earth where Timothy was now waiting for me, and we began to heal my relationship with human men on this 3D plane. In my own experience, I had concluded that men were unreliable and couldn't be trusted. I projected this belief everywhere, especially toward God. Like that fog lifting on a dewy morning; when my internal state shifted, my projection did, too. I saw everything for what it was and got to work on cleaning up my head and heart, quickly.

I dissected my dad stuff. I resolved issues about exes. I explored my resentment for the patriarchy. I voiced my disappointment with the government, DMV, and the post office. Y'all, I got thorough about my unhealed wounds around the masculine energy that exists in the third dimension. I left no stone unturned. I dug up everything I could and discovered gunk I didn't know existed in me, and it was such a relief to clear it all out.

In my commitment to a thriving sense of self, relationships, business, marriage, and future, I was willing to take on all the work there was to do to be in complete integrity, alignment, and faith. It was worth it to have the fullest life in service of the highest good of all. It is due to this breakthrough that the floodgates of abundance were opened and this book slid down my golden thread from the fifth dimension, straight to your hands. Thank God for Timothy and thank God for God. No matter how you relate to him, he is omnipotent and benevolent, and he patiently awaits your permission to bless you beyond your wildest dreams.

Speaking of being blessed beyond your wildest dreams, let's talk about what it looks like for you to recreate your relationship with your Higher Power. Based on my own share, I want to give you a few things to consider that will begin breaking down your barriers. I am not writing this to convince or coerce you into a relationship with anyone or anything you are not open to. If you are, great. As the title promises, this is a guide back to Love. There is plenty to get from this pillar even if you do not feel fully ready to come home to your Higher Power. This book will read a lot differently if and when you are ready. This pillar will also have a lot of powerful insights, messages, and tools for you to utilize, even if that just means being a more loving human on the planet. Take whatever serves you and leave what you wish. Writing to reach the hearts of thousands on this topic is an invitation I accepted. I will do my best to fulfill my word and guide you back to Love.

Taking on this work can grant you access to Love unlike anything on this 3D plane. Sure, we all have our humans who love, adore, and care for us, and they are human too. They take days off, have their own stuff, live their own lives, and deal with challenges of their own. No human can love as wholly and fully as our Source Energy can. It is an unwavering, eternal nucleus of energy radiating everything you could ever possibly need at all times, without fail. You don't have to ask for it, you don't have to earn it, there are no requirements to feel the love of God. He just lovingly waits with open arms for you to turn back to him. He is always holding out your golden thread to you, and you may grab on and let go a million times over in this lifetime, yet his offering of love and forgiveness will never change.

It is we who must change. It is we who must turn back to him. Timothy taught me that 'to repent' means to turn. With my Catholic background, I was accustomed to 'penance' and felt the need to be ashamed and beg for the forgiveness and love of God. This is not exactly necessary. As humans with a conscience, we may desire to make amends in our lives, but this is about us, not about God. To simply turn away from anything that is not Love, turn back, and lean in, is all that needs to happen for us to be welcomed back into experiencing God's graces. His grace is always available. He is always right behind us. It is we who pinch ourselves off from that flow of abundance. It is we who choose to turn back whenever and however many times we do.

Your relationship with a Higher Power will become

important at some point in your life. The more you ignore it, the more obvious and in your face it will become. I share in the Integrity Pillar that what you resist persists, and it will become so apparent that you will not be able to ignore it. Your subconscious communications will manifest as constant invitations to turn back to Love. God was working directly through Timothy, with very little subtlety, to invite me back. He used a human, who could speak clear English to me, to personally ask me back. It was my job to accept, and Timothy had a pretty graceful way about him that made that choice simple, comfortable, and the greatest relief of my life. The sooner you honor the invitations to heal your relationship with God, the sooner you get to receive all the blessings of an abundant and peaceful life.

I hope this reading inspires you to live your life with your eyes up, ears on, and heart open to the invitations to return to Love. It is a beautiful life to live. It is an amazing gift to have and to give away and it is available at all times.

What really makes this gift available at all times is through your efforts of deconditioning yourself from the impact of the third dimensional reality. It can be really heavy and challenging down here and that can distract even some of the most faithful human beings. Being born and raised in an environment where love is seldom available or worse, judgment of all types is thriving, can prevent a human from ever consciously turning to their Source in this lifetime. People are born and die without ever knowing a force greater than them and while this doesn't make them bad people, simply existing in one dimension limits their options and resources. This is not to condemn. This is an offer. It is an invitation to tap into that wellspring of multidimensional abundance that co-creates with you on this plane.

One belief that I had to decondition myself from was the idea that I was all alone here on the planet. I had made one of my motivational mantras, "you are born alone and you will die alone" to keep me working really hard to achieve what I thought I wanted in life. From this solo mindset, I forced outcomes, manipulated factors, pushed and pulled, and just plain overworked for things that were simple to attain and create. Because I felt alone, I felt a deep sadness and dissatisfaction by many of my achievements, regardless of the success. I didn't have anyone to really share them with. I felt alone on a deep level.

Whenever I felt alone, I would try to tap into my Grammy Rose Guardian Angel, and it worked in its own right. I felt a breath of support and guidance, but it wasn't consistently present in my life in a way that helped me fully relax. I still felt like if anything were to get done in my life, I was going to have to work really hard for it to happen. This was an exhausting, discouraging, and disempowering belief to maintain for extended periods of time. The idea of keeping this up for life seemed pretty unbearable and unrealistic.

I became way more willing to decondition all of my disbelief once I felt that homecoming hug from

God. Hear me out when I say this: just because I felt his love and presence doesn't mean I fully understood how to release decades of fear and distrust. My human heart had a lot of experiences and evidence about why God was unreliable and couldn't be trusted. Even after months of practice from that breakthrough, I had to catch myself turning away from God out of habit or self-preservation.

My greatest practice actually came in the form of Timothy, as well. During this time, we became so aligned in our humanness that the love of God felt like the fire-hose of abundance once we open ourselves up to Love. Believing and maintaining the concept that men are unreliable definitely got in the way of me fully trusting that Timothy wouldn't break my heart, like so many had before. We both defaulted to self-preservation survival mechanisms in the beginning of our relationship, not because of anything we did to each other, but as a result of being dead scared of being disappointed, yet again.

It was so beneficial that we were both coaches who could recognize our own and each other's survival patterns and were able to address them while they were in operation. This awareness prevented us from sabotaging the relationship with the most predictable fear of all time, "this is too good to be true." We both agreed this wouldn't come between us and allowed our relationship to be great. We allowed ourselves to love and be loved. We allowed abundance to wash over us individually, as well as together, and supported each other in the expansion of our capacity for blessings.

Don't get it twisted, abundance can be uncomfortable. We have been made to believe that we are undeserving, flawed, broken, unworthy, and more. We have so many unconscious reflexes to deflect abundance strictly because of the discomfort of receiving. Too many blessings coming at us with such ease and flow literally feels foreign, and wrong to us on a cellular level. This tricks us into sabotaging our prosperity just so we can level back into what's familiar; average, moderate, mundane, and mediocre. We know what to do with those feelings and modes of operation. We don't exactly know how to act when extraordinary experiences are constantly available. We must recondition ourselves to be able to receive a larger capacity of amazingness and be okay with it.

Timothy and I being committed to this realization empowered us to hold that kind of possibility for each other and anyone else. It is what has me teaching this to you right now. I feel so blessed by this because I am well aware that this is not true for everyone and every relationship. I am committed to giving you as many tools as possible in this book to utilize in your own life to make room for the most extraordinary experience you can humanly tolerate.

Based on so much information from the Integrity Pillar, we know that people act and react unconsciously in life and constantly repel blessings as a byproduct of conditioned scarcity, lack of faith, and heartbreak. We do this automatically, but now you know it doesn't have to be that way. You do not have to subscribe to the beliefs that life is hard, people are awful, and everything is hopeless just to condition your heart not to experience hurt. It is a bass ackwards approach to protecting yourself from pain. I hope our story opens you up to consider how you may be blocking abundance and sabotaging your success as a result of past fear, hurt, and trauma.

I wanted to begin this chapter by telling my spiritual story in full detail because I believe it will make many lessons of the Faith Pillar fluid from this point. I learn and teach best through example, and I think these rather intangible concepts are most easily understood in the third dimension through with 3D examples, so let's give this a go. I want to dive face first into faith by explaining the mystical wonders of trust and surrender.

As per usual, I will be taking the magic and mysticism out of these two concepts, because I think these important aspects of faith are often lost upon us, even if we are committed to practicing them. Before I begin sharing a few invitations, I want to lay a thick foundational belief that I implore you to live by: you can have it all.

If I had a nickel for how many times people tried to convince me that I would have to compromise the fullest vision of my life, I'd be a millionaire, solely through that. And at some points, I have compromised it. Early in my life, I did not truly believe that I could live in Southern California, work for myself when, how, and where I want, much less with whom I want, and make as much as I want. I especially did not think that I'd be able to do this while also traveling, writing books, having the relationship of my dreams, and building a global company that positively impacts people and supports them living their absolute best life! That was not a reality for me; that was a movie scene. I had been coming to California since childhood and always assumed that if I ever let myself move here, I would be a broke, beach bum because I would never want to work or take life seriously. I stopped myself from chasing my dreams because I didn't trust myself to have them. You too have dreams that you don't trust yourself with.

I even settled for a different dream when I married my college sweetheart and planned to settle down in the Midwest to have a family and live a corporate employee, suburban lifestyle. There is absolutely wrong with that lifestyle and one point, I thought it would be my best life. What I knew and ignored was that I was no nine-to-fiver, and I am not built for winter! God had more perspective than I and removed that marriage from my life. I had some healing to do but I mostly understood that this was a second chance at life and love, and I promised myself not to squander the lesson or opportunity. After a year of recovery work, I had that integrity rampage, packed my Jeep, and drove off to the best coast...I mean the West Coast.

After making my inner work the number one priority in my life, I understood on an intellectual level that you can, in fact, have it all. I want to be careful about this statement because so many people confuse this for greed, selfishness, or material obsession, and that is the furthest from what I am talking about. The 'having it all' I am referring to is in the realm of peace, bliss, love, abundance, connection, joy, gratitude, faith, guidance, trust, communication, and limitlessness.

To better explain how that looks 'in the real world,' your 'all' doesn't look like anyone else's. Even the 'having it all' of your past, isn't the same as the 'all' of your future. By nature of the Law of Attraction, once you attain certain things, you will notice a contrast and upgrade your desires, naturally leaving some things behind and refining your vision. 'Having it all' may look like some material things, of course, we came here to fully experience this life. But we also came here to fully engage in our existence, meaning that 'having it all' may look like having very little and enjoying every minute you are here. You will have your own definition of 'having it all,' and your heart will tell you when it is full, or help you identify what is missing.

This definition will require you doing the inner work of knowing your own version of satisfaction and success. If you learn how to listen within, this 'having it all' will be in alignment with the highest good of all and will also be a contribution to the Collective. This is about fulfilling our roles as cells in the body of humanity and purpose. Some even consider this honoring God's will. However you think of it, you will feel divinely led down this path.

This, my friend, is where trust and surrender become the most important skills you have. I want to be so clear when I tell you that you are galactically cared for, protected, provided for, and loved. You are never alone and you always have a universe of resources available to you. To trust this truth will open up the floodgates for you. Trust is about relaxing into the knowledge that what you have asked for is here or on its way. Ask, and it will be given. Ask, and you shall receive. From here, your responsibility is to surrender how it will show up in physical form, and live with those eyes up, ears on, and heart open, ready to receive.

There is a bit of a trick to this because when you ask for patience, you are given opportunities to practice patience. This means that these opportunities will test your patience and feel like the opposite of what you asked for. This trains and conditions you to be patient.

Another example is praying for the gift of being calm. You will be put into situations to practice being calm, cool, and collected. This means that these opportunities will test your balance and feel like the opposite of what you asked for. This trains and conditions you to be calm in any situation because you have a new point of reference.

One more, because this is fun. When you ask for money and to be rich, you will be put into circumstances that teach you what it feels like to not have money and to appreciate, manage, and respect it. This means that these opportunities will test your money management and feel like the opposite of what you asked for. This trains and conditions you to honor your wealth because you have a full understanding of what it takes to be wealthy.

We learn through our own experiences. Even now, as I share all of this information that you may understand intellectually, you will not internalize these lessons until you walk through them yourself. Your own trials and errors will solidify your inner authority, and you will learn to trust your internal guidance system.

Your internal guidance system is your intuition, and that is in union with The Source. Gut feelings, intuitive hits, and pings of inspiration are all tugs on your golden thread from the divine. Your skill in trust and surrender lies in quieting the outside world, to listen to the inner one. You must trust that what you hear from within is perfect for you, and you must constantly give up that your ego self; your thinking brain, knows better than the whispers of your heart.

Surrender is about giving up your self identity to trust and honor what you hear. This can be a bit scary and uncertain as you get started. It takes courage, but as discussed in the Alignment Pillar, there are ways to strengthen this skill, and even master it. Something you will have to do on a conscious level is practice patience, acceptance, and forgiveness of your own humanness.

This is where Transcendence joins the show. When you are operating with full levels of trust, constantly surrendering to divine guidance, and forgiving the human self for its humanness, you will practically be levitating through life. This is not in a 'better than' kind of way. This is in a full-blown leadership kind of way. This is in a purely inspired kind of way. This is the complete embodiment of being an Alchemist, and people will be able to witness The Source of Love in your presence.

If you commit to trusting and surrendering on a moment-to-moment basis, you will transcend and lead people home, effortlessly. You will be living an extraordinary life filled with and fueled by love. You will be thriving in service of the highest good of all and I can promise you that whatever definition of abundance lies in your heart of hearts, you will certainly be having it all.

Chapter 17

Love, Acceptance, and Self-Expression

You may find yourself kind of surprised by the foundation of faith that I lay out in this pillar, because it is primarily based upon faith in oneself. I have spent large portions of this book explaining that The Source is Love and that every single thing in existence is an extension of that Love energy; that includes you. You are an expression of all that is. You are God. You are the Universe. You are The Source. You have that level of potential power.

As you can probably imagine, I am not referencing power in general. I am referencing personal power. More specifically, I am referring to individual sovereignty, which is the ability to govern oneself. In relation to faith, this means fully accepting the unlimited access to power from within, and honing, harnessing, and directing that energy effectively for the HGA.

Fully examining the inner self to discover, develop, and master this version of you will lead to self-actualization, which is the realization and fulfillment of one's gifts, purpose, and mission here. What you are tasked with is fully comprehending your particular challenges in this lifetime, as well as how you will shift them into your personal brand of leadership. Self-actualization is about releasing everything you are not, in order to fully embody all that you came here to be.

Becoming the fullest version of yourself is a natural evolution and in some ways, it is a linear process of aging and a quantum process of maturation. I'm sure we can all agree that age does not equal maturity. We all have vastly different timelines in life that expose us to different things at different times. Keep in mind, you came here for this. Your soul agreed to this round before taking a body and although you may not remember that, trying that theory on for size doesn't hurt either.

Accepting what has happened to you in your life can shift you into gratitude for those experiences. This is a secret key that unlocks your freedom to use your life lessons to step up as the unique leader that you are. It is only here that you can mature into the fullest expression of your divine leadership. To understand that what you have faced has specifically chiseled and polished you to govern yourself is a great tool of inner authority, and helps you develop the skills needed to be here for the highest good of all.

It takes incredible faith to embody every part of you. Many things have occurred in our lives that we would rather not share. There are parts of us that we may feel ashamed of. It takes meeting every part of you to embody every part of you. As shared in depth in the integration chapter, we must fully see, know, accept, love, and share every facet of us to truly appreciate the multidimensional gem that we are and deliver our gifts to this world. Integrating that we have many sides makes us versatile in our ability to serve here without being negatively impacted by factors of the third dimension. It also makes us relatable to those we serve who are struggling with similar aspects of humanness. Constantly remembering that we are energetic beings having a human experience allows us to transcend any and all barriers to being radiant light beings, leading the way to our lasting peace.

To be here powerfully, without this world dimming your light, will require faith in the Source. It isn't a matter of if that Source is available, faith in The Source and your direct connection to it is a learned skill. It is a trained mental and emotional muscle that increases your endurance to keep showing up for the HGA.

My invitation and challenge to you is to accept yourself so fully that you are yourself in the most unabashed, unapologetic type of way. Knowing, loving, and accepting yourself completely is an imperative aspect of your duty on this planet, because this allows for our humanness, while not being fully operated by it. This is a great example to set for others because it can inspire them to begin the work of introspection, acceptance, and sovereignty. Being human is one aspect of us. Being an extraordinary expression of love is another aspect. Which of those we honor more will directly determine the quality and direction of our life. This will also directly impact the rate at which humanity takes arriving back to the Garden state.

Each and every one of us plays an intricate and important role in our Collective atonement. Quite frankly, if you are not a part of the solution, you are a part of the problem. I usually take issue with that previous statement but I want you to realize that you are always either contributing to the Cycle of Hurt or Love. There are no breaks from this. If you are not constantly contributing to the Cycle of Love, you are slowing us down. We cannot get there separately. We are not separate. We will not get there until every last one of us crosses that finish line.

I also take issue with making that statement because what there is to understand about transformation is that even the dark stuff has its place and purpose. There are no mistakes in this Universe, and so someone acting out or selfishly causes a chain of events that will in some way contribute to our evolution. However, we were born with free will and our arrival back to peace will take us as long as it takes until we are all operating with love, cooperation, and interdependence.

This will require each of us being connected to The Source energy and respecting that the use of power for dominance in the 3D harms the Collective. It is through our connection to our core spirit that we know we are abundant beings and surrender our need for excess.

We are cared for, provided for, protected, and loved, and when everyone can settle into that knowledge and reach that level of maturity, we can coexist powerfully and equally. It is our disconnection from our core that divides us. We must operate together in connection. This will create a mutual understanding, appreciation, and respect for one another that can usher in times of peace, bliss, and joy.

On the level of self, it is your job to keep all of this knowledge at the forefront of your mind on a moment-to-moment basis. The term 'namaste' means the greatness in me recognizes the greatness in you. The Tao Te Ching reminds us that once you see the face of God, you recognize it in every face you see. It will be through the process of your own inner work that you will be able to freely access and unleash the greatness in everyone you meet. This will cause you to alchemize judgment and darkness in others before they sense it within themselves. Being a whole and complete human being that can integrate your energetic self in this 3D field will be upcycling darkness in the world and alleviating us all.

Living this way in the world will become an example for others of their potential to be powerful alchemists as well. A great part of this is that when you are winning the game of life with strong integrity, alignment, and faith, alchemizing even some of the heaviest and darkest energy for others will feel like lifting feathers for you. With strong endurance and immunity, you will be alchemizing at a rapid rate and contributing to our fast approaching freedom.

Now, imagine how your example will lead more and more people home to Love. Directly and indirectly training others will turn the tide for the Collective. Think of how many people will shift by reading this book. Think of the ripple effect of it. Consider all the powerful light beings doing this same work, and more. Imagine all the warriors of Love in the world moving massive amounts of energy to create our momentum in the Cycle of Love.

Even if your daily task to start is to not contribute to the Cycle of Hurt, you are fulfilling an important role as an Alchemist. That contribution supports all the folks who are transmuting large, energetic barriers that stand between us and the Garden State. Keep the faith in where we are headed. Hold the vision of peace in your mind's eye. Visualize harmony in your meditations and dreams. Every positive reinforcement of our future matters and your contribution matters every moment of every day.

Thank you for your contribution to the evolution of humanity. Namaste.

Chapter 18

Divine Feminine and Masculine Leadership

I am bouncing up and down in the back of my Jeep with enthusiasm to be writing this chapter! I even wrote out five lines consisting of "thank you" before starting this first sentence. This topic is so special to me personally and is one of the most misunderstood aspects of our humanity. Fully respecting the feminine and masculine energies for what they are and have to offer is important in our roles here. It is instrumental in our leadership and is one of the most subtle factors that contributes to how true Transcendence really occurs in this realm.

Understanding the divine feminine and masculine, aka DFM, is as important as being a mechanic and understanding how a car engine works. It is absolutely necessary for the work to be done correctly. To grasp the concept of DFM means you understand all of our natural states of being and can honor our functionality.

Without this comprehension and application of this knowledge, we are limiting our option to operate at full capacity. Reaching our potential is unequivocally reliant upon each individual internalizing this wisdom for themselves.

We can afford to and would be greatly served to be teaching this information to our people at a much younger age, and I have faith that over time, it will be integrated into developmental education. Too early, we are reinforcing the 'pink is for girls' and 'blue is for boys' types of gender identities that limit any human's potential to tap into their wellspring of infinite intelligence. We nearly start a child's life eliminating fifty percent of their access to expression.

To teach gender roles over the aspects of masculinity and femininity brings this concept crashing face first into the third dimension, where there is no magic or possibility, only concrete and definitive reality. As we have evolved, we have created a sliding scale of gender fluidity and while it is progress, it is still pretty limited to the 3D. We are still only discussing the physiological make-up of a human being in many cases and overstepping what is occurring energetically for people. This is a conversation that must be refined if we are going to evolve into reaching the highest good of all.

In a few cultures, especially that of Native Americans, there is considered to be five main genders: masculine men, feminine men, masculine women, feminine women, and two-spirits. It is likely that you can imagine people you know who fit all of these gender identities.

You also probably know immediately which one you identify with.

Within each population, these different gender identities tend to fulfill roles in alignment with their contribution to the Collective. We see the masculine men as hunters, warriors, and fathers. We see feminine men step up as guides, philosophers, spiritual leaders, and townsmen. We see masculine women as gatherers and warriors in their own right, and taking roles in the workforce. We see feminine women as mothers, care-givers, and other supportive roles.

Two-spirited individuals have an ambiguity about them that keeps them actively on the middle ground between male and female. They have a wider range of options and wider gap between limitations. They are versatile in the application of one or both identities and this can be both accepted and rejected by themselves and others. Specifically in Western culture, this identity has been confusing for people in the past. Due to the innovation of the Information Age, ambiguity has been normalized and is more widely understood.

To begin integrating our DFM, we must make a shift from prioritizing gender to focusing on the ener-getic presence of a human being. In the 3D reality, I am an advocate for the whole spectrum of this experience. For example, I am in full support of someone transi-tioning to the opposite gender, *and* I believe that there is much inner work to be done before drawing the con-clusion that adjusting the physical make-up of the body will be the best expression of the inner state of being.

For example, not every masculine female needs to transition physically in order to embody and celebrate their masculinity, and the same goes for feminine men. We need individuals in their originally chosen bodies to fulfill their unique roles as they are. I also acknowledge our transgender brothers and sisters for their contribution to our evolution of reconfiguring our relationship to gender identity in this time space reality. They have innovated our ways of thinking, being, acting, and reacting. They have stretched us beyond the physical to consider the energetic identity of an individual and expanded our ability to accept one another. This has been such an important brick in the road of humanity's path. It is certainly moving us forward.

Moving on past gender, let's further discuss the identities of the divine feminine and masculine energies. To start, I would like to make a distinction between being wounded and healed. This applies to both the feminine and masculine and knowing how it shows up in our character will empower all of us to consciously identify and be at choice about our impact in the world.

This takes us back to the Integrity Pillar and the concepts of being complete, taking responsibility for ourselves, healing our trauma, and integrating our shadow. Unhealed feminine and masculine beings are out in the world unconsciously contributing to the Cycle of Hurt. They are projecting their pain instead of alchemizing it and in many senses, making more work for others. I once read a quote that signifies this example of the wounded energies; "someone's therapist knows all about you."

Ouch. To be someone causing another person's trauma is an obvious indicator of your own. This is a clear indicator that you are out there functioning as the unhealed feminine or masculine. Before I share some of the characteristics of the unhealed energies, I want to invite you to drop your 3D gender identity and explore both your feminine and masculine selves. Even in the five genders I explained, all have both energies. We all have both energies. Being able to observe them fully will give you full facility over your whole self.

The unhealed masculine has characteristics commonly referred to as 'toxic masculinity.' This phrase has become more mainstream over time but many don't actually know the full scope of what that entails. Some characteristics of the unhealed masculine include:

- Competitive
- Confrontational
- Predatory
- Abusive
- Dominant
- Controlling
- Critical
- Aggressive
- Unstable
- Unsupportive
- Cowardly
- Dishonest
- Impulsive
- Egocentric

These are just a few of the most obvious examples

of what the unhealed masculine energy looks like in the world. Again, keep in mind that this energy can show up in a man or woman. We know competitive, dominant women. This is a sign of holding trauma in her masculine energy that has gone unidentified or has not been tended to. This is equally as important to witness in all genders. It is important for all humans to heal both of their energies.

Examples of unhealed feminine energy includes:

- Withdrawn
- Manipulative
- Jealous
- Avoidant
- Victimized
- Powerless
- Weak
- Submissive
- Needy
- Co-dependent
- Overly sensitive
- Overly emotional
- Insecure
- Inauthentic

These are predictably recognizable as wounded feminine energy when pointed out and can be embodied by both men and women. The wounded energies disempower an individual from tapping into the most authentic versions of themselves and certainly prevent them from living out their leadership. When it comes to gender, transgender, and gender roles, no one is really at choice about who they are or want to be when they are operating from the unhealed energies.

Transformational growth is the initial, essential work for any individual to do before making decisions about gender associations, vocations, or roles in life. All too often we choose the entire course of our life from the unhealed energies. It is our responsibility to take on self discovery, development, and mastery to transcend any singular identity that inhibits our expression of the divine.

To shift into the divine, we must learn the characteristics of the healed masculine and feminine energies. The healed masculine characteristics are as follows:

- Protective
- Confident
- Humble
- Helpful
- Responsible
- Focused
- Clear
- Logical
- Supportive
- Active
- Giving
- Stable
- Direct
- Certain
- Expansive
- Assertive
- Capable

- Disciplined
- Courageous
- Present
- Articulate
- Secure

I don't know about you but just reading over this list makes me feel good. It's like a breath of fresh air to imagine a being this way. We have established that this healed masculine energy applies to both men and women, so I will start referencing them more specifically as the 'divine' energies from this point. A healed person is a divine person. A healed person is tapped into the divine source of infinite intelligence and provides the understanding that transcends physicality.

More people elevating above a gender identity to tap into the divine masculine would provide so much for the world. There would be an unprecedented presence of stability, honesty, and reliability that would remove so much pain and insecurity that plagues our population. People would feel held and supported to thrive interdependently with the divine masculine functioning at full force.

Healing our own masculine energy is an important task to take on as an alchemist. Imagine clearing your head and heart space of all trauma, fear, and judgment, to represent this list above. You would be unbelievably powerful and unstoppable in your purpose for the highest good of all. You would certainly have access to your greatest life as your greatest self.

The different identities of God and the example of

Jesus are the most reliable representations of the divine masculine incarnate, to be models for you to fulfill this role. To embody the everlasting love of God will empower you to hold space for so much on this plane. You will occur like a cornerstone for many to center themselves on your stabilizing energy. You will serve the world as a foundational being and a house of protection.

To make sure we incorporate every facet of your greatest self to manifest your greatest life, let's explore the aspects of the healed, divine feminine:

- Receptive
- Tender
- Passive
- Kind
- Sensitive
- Still
- Intuitive
- Loving
- Understanding
- Nurturing
- Flowing
- Radiant
- Surrendered
- Emotional
- Full of ease
- Graceful
- Allowing
- Forgiving

Again, what a breath of fresh air to imagine such a fully feminine being in your presence. This is the type of being who can heal the planet. The alchemy that can be performed by this type of person can alleviate humanity from some of its most painful suffering.

In the beginning of this book, I reference my Guardian Angel energy. For me, this is cognitively the highest state of being I have access to. It allows me to tap into my divine femininity, which in turn, grants me access to my sovereignty. This supports my ability to show up faithfully in the world to make an impact in alignment with the highest good of all. It is my Guardian Angel identity that I personally identify with to embody this list above.

Another divine feminine identity to tap into is Mother Nature. When holding space for the weather of this world, Mother Nature is unshakable to her core. She is ever adaptive, passive, forgiving, and expansive. Her flexibility keeps her nimble in the ever-evolving world and yet it is her firmly planted roots that keep her grounded.

To embody both energies of DFM, a human has limitless potential to alchemize anything in this world. This kind of elevation moves mountains. This stage of Transcendence accounts for unshakable faith in the divine. In this energetic space, anything is possible; including humanity's arrival back to peace.

Recognition and reverence for both energies within each human being is what will unlock our potential to access harmony amongst each other. It will take healing each person and then elevating into his/her own leadership to fulfill their role as a cell in the body of humanity and lay their brick in the forward direction.

This is all possible. It will take our interdependence to reach this Garden State and I just want to keep repeating; it is possible. I would like to bring in one final aspect of how we can attain such bliss. Understanding how to co-create with each other and our Higher Powers is what will bring these visions to fruition.

In reference to the DFM, I am going to bring the two apart again into gender identities as to bring them back into the 3D. I have been repeating it this whole book, this knowledge is for you to apply in your day to day, not tuck it away on your bookshelf when you finish this final page. I didn't type my fingers numb because I think this is just a good idea. I wrote a guidebook to guide; for it to be applied.

I want to take a moment to share what this looks like from the perspective of gender roles. My favorite analogy for this is women are water and men are the container. Let's use a riverbed as the container for the men for this example. Women flow. We wash left and right and move up and down. Our tides shift with the push and pull of the moon and we are very dynamic in our natural state of being.

Men are sturdy and reliable. They can hold and support women as their energies sway to and fro. With man as the riverbed, their bends lead and guide the woman to her desired destination with ease, grace, and effortless flow. This is a collaboration amongst the two; a divine dance of the feminine and masculine energies.

Timothy loves to remind me that the woman commands and the man leads. Women are creative beings and so we hold the vision while the man paves the path and leads the way. Men support and provide and thrive in their leadership along the journey. This is the marriage of the divine masculine and feminine. This is teamwork, partnership, commitment, faith, trust, and surrender to each other in service of the HGA.

In alignment with interdependence, we are better together. There is absolutely no need or expectation to do this work alone. It is more fun, fluid, and faster to collaborate and cooperate in our endeavor toward the Garden State. It will certainly be rewarding to arrive there together, as well.

So here I say unto you, my dear. Take the most you can of the DFM and apply them to your identity in this physical realm. Be as much of both as you can and take on the inner work of the Integrity and Alignment Pillars to embody the full DFM as you continue to transcend. This is your work in the world. The rest of what there is to be, do, and have will reveal itself to you over time. This is where your intuition and faith play such a major role.

It will take profound levels of faith to see and hear your inner guidance so clearly that you can access it on a moment-to-moment basis to live, plan, act, and react from your highest and best at all times. Freedom and courage to choose is a byproduct of being fully tapped into and embodying the DFM.

For even more information on how to do this, you can tune into the Divine Feminine & Masculine Series on my Hearts Unleashed Podcast. In the episodes of this series, I dive deep into mastery level integration of the DFM into your everyday life.

This work is pure magic. How fascinating it is to witness people come to me, frantic and frazzled by unhealed energies, and leave their coaching experience grounded in their divinity and sovereignty. It is alchemy at its finest.

You have unlimited resources and potential available to you and what you can create with it will absolutely heal the planet. Do not hesitate any longer to start practicing faith in the infinite access to peace, bliss, joy, love, and creation.

Chapter 19

Intuition

Wowzers, my people. We are arriving at the end of our journey soon; at least for now. Before we part, I'd like to help you polish your intuitive skill set so you can be one sharp alchemist out there. Faith in your senses is one of the greatest gifts you can possess, so I encourage you to check back in with this guide every once in a while to gauge your evolution and recalibrate to your next level of elevation.

Being a trained alchemist in the third dimension can sometimes feel like having a certification in wizardry from Hogwarts. It's fun, it's fancy, and it's freeing. Having heightened senses and levels of awareness will have you reading energies and unspoken messages from every direction. It's fascinating and often causes blissful out-of-body experiences.

As people begin developing these skills, they begin experiencing deja-vu for a while. There is a sense of "I've been here before," or "I know this," or "I've seen this before." This is you being super tapped in and fluid between all of the dimensions. Enjoy the ride!

This definitely takes some getting used to and can cause a little bit of a vertigo sensation I like to call an 'awareness hangover,' much like rocking back and forth on a cruise ship headed straight for the Bermuda Triangle. Don't fret though, you will get your footing eventually, and once you do, you will be standing on the firm foundation of your intuition.

Think about all the material we covered in this book. If you take on all the work offered to you, you will have such a powerful sense of self that you will truly understand that you are the same God consciousness you once didn't fully understand. You are The Source Energy that you came from and will go back to. You are Infinite Intelligence with infinite intelligence to pull from.

I highlight all of this to say that you have the magnetism of the North and South Poles combined. You can stir up the energy of the galaxies for the sake of creation and manifest anything you desire. You can communicate telepathically to call in anything from anywhere on the planet. This is the Law of Attraction in action and if you stay committed to the work of this guidebook, you will become a master of transcending humanness and alchemizing energy.

So, let's have a little orientation for your newly unleashed heart. Have you ever heard the quote "with great power, comes great responsibility?" It has a lot of truth to it. You have a responsibility to use all of this wisdom for good, not evil; for light, not darkness. It is a part of your divine destiny to be a contribution in your time here and my request is that you are always contributing to the Cycle of Love.

If you have read this way through this entire book, my guess is that you fully understand that you were made for more. Your soul took a body in which to do impactful things and leave a legacy of transformative momentum. What that may likely look like is what I refer to as 'Love movements.' These are the movements, companies, non-for-profits, drives, groups, events, charities, and many more that unleashed hearts create in the world as an expression of their contribution and love.

It is when people discover what they are truly passionate about that they create their life around it. One of my favorite phrases is 'healed people, heal people.' Love movements of every kind are healed people following through on their clear intuitive guidance as to what they came here to do for the highest good of all.

One thing I want to say about this is that the scale on which your love movement impacts the Collective can be whatever it naturally is. You don't have to have some million dollar idea or start an international company to launch your love movement. Your heart will communicate it to you, and my guess is that you have had the vision in your head your entire life. My other guess is that you just never followed through on it until now.

Now you have an entire guidebook to help you remove the blocks, barriers, and gunk, manifest your love movement, and create your dreams. I want to sprinkle some extra hope and excitement on your plans by explaining that once you energetically commit to following through with your vision, the Universe starts celebrating with you.

God gets so excited when his beings begin chasing their dreams. When you show up to answer the call of divine inspiration, there will most certainly be divine intervention. You'd better buckle up at this point because the blessings will begin to rain and the firehouse of abundance will blast you right in the face! Recall how Timothy and I had to support each other in expanding our capacity to receive Love so fully? This will be a task you must take on as well, so that you do not sabotage your dreams out of fear or run out of emotional endurance to keep up with the pace as the Universe fast tracks your desires.

The longer you have waited in life to fulfill your purpose is how multiplied your prosperity will be if you fully surrender to your calling. Your Spirit will be up in the fifth dimension doing a happy dance, maybe even an Irish jig, over you finally standing up for what you believe in. Your higher self will be jingling every golden thread of every co-creative component in this world for you to have everything you need at your disposal to create your love movement and get it off the ground.

You'd better lace up your running shoes for this marathon because every Guardian Angel, Spirit Guide, Ancestor, passed Loved One, and good God himself will be joining you in your race to the finish line. This life is meant to be so much fun, my dear reader. Shed absolutely everything that is not for you, master yourself, and unleash your big ol' heart on this world. We need you out here in the game of life. We've been waiting. Join in. The water's fine.

Chapter 20

Winning the Game of Life

We have made it full circle in our adventure here, my love. I want to leave you with a few parting words, invitations, and congratulations for taking this journey with me. Although these pages may come to an end, your endeavors are far from over. Your quest continues and now you have a full understanding that you are the captain of your ship.

Never be afraid to be the pure, divine, incredible leader that you are. We need you out there. I need you out there. God needs you out there. You need you out there. I know you know the joy you will feel when you are living life unleashed, and you have every right to enjoy this life you've got. Make the most of it. Thank you again, for investing your time and energy in becoming an alchemist. I honor you.

May your travels be blessed,
and your days be bright.

May your feet be swift,
and your heart be light.

May you know yourself and God,
and believe in both fully.

May you follow your heart,
and be yourself truly.

May you find truth and Love,
at the core of all that is.

May you share that truth with all,
with faith, joy, and bliss.

For it is out in this world,
that so many get lost.

But we know where home is
and it doesn't come at a cost.

No matter how far off we stray
we can always come back.

We can turn right back to God
and always get on track.

Do not ever lose faith, my dear
there is always hope.

Stay in integrity and alignment
when you forget how to cope.

There is always a way, child,
there is always guidance from above.

When you alchemize judgment
you will make your way back to Love.

With Love~ Jill, Rhonda, & Abigail

To Our Dear Readers,

We at Hearts Unleashed are so grateful to serve you.

Thank you for opening your heart up to receive the message of this book & to take your light out into the world. We are dedicated to your mental, emotion, & spiritual freedom. We are here for you every step of the way.

In great love,
The Hearts Unleashed Team

Acknowledgments

To life, love, and all that is possible. To this infinite Universe and our ever-expanding consciousness. May we always lean into all that it has to offer.

To my clients, past, present, and future. I acknowledge your commitment to living out your purpose and fullest life. I am honored to walk with you on any part of your journey and am grateful for you joining me in mine. What a gift it is to live out loud and watch our ripple effect have such a positive impact on the world. You are so important and I am grateful for the way you show up for this work. Keep sharing, keep shining.

To my best friend of decades, Rachel. You are the greatest, most loyal friend and I am forever grateful for your love. You have held me through my darkest days and cheered me on in every way. You are hilarious, beautiful, inspiring, and a light in this world.

You showed me God before I had ever met him and taught me how to pray. You showed me what compassion and connection are and have provided both since the day we met. You brought me closer to the divine and I see your connection to it in your smile, laughter, and hugs. I love you endlessly, Rachie. I thank God for you daily.

To my kind, gentle, adorable, intelligent, and compassionate husband, Timothy. You have transformed my life and I will gladly share it with you for the rest of our days. Thank you for helping me heal my relationship with man and God. Thank you for bringing me closer to my own divinity and sovereignty. I honor you and am in awe of the vessel of love you are for mankind.

Thank you for listening beyond my words and seeing beyond what's in front of you. Your spirit is so big and I love witnessing you in your brilliance. I acknowledge you for honoring your guidance and call to serve and heal. You are an integral leader at a time we need you most.

You are one of the sweetest souls I know and I am glad we get to play human together.

Thank you forever,
Abigail

About the Author

"Abby is truly an example of someone living a life they love. Her ability to create that connection through her writing is a beautiful gift. She is a powerful author and an even more powerful person. If you want to get out of your own way and make something happen, start with this book."

—Review of Abigail's first book,
Giving Up Giving Up: The Memoir of a Quitter

Heart-centered entrepreneur, Abigail Gazda has transformed her passion for education into a full-time career as a motivational speaker, author, and life coach. She is the CEO of Hearts Unleashed, a full-service transformation company committed to empowering people to operate with full freedom, power, and self expression in every area of life.

Abigail is a Clarity Coach and supports souls speaking up about their silent struggle and unleashing the authentic leader within. As the host of the Hearts Unleashed Podcast, she is committed to turning dreamers into doers and helping raise the frequency of humanity with the development of Emotional Intelligence.

As a best-selling author, Abigail's relatable way of sharing sheds light to what we instinctively know by putting words to what has gone previously unidentified within us. She speaks to the soul through truth, and challenges you to consider new perspectives. Her invitations will ground you into your own internal knowledge, and inspire you to live your heart unleashed.

Born and raised a proud Indiana Hoosier, Abigail currently resides and surfs in Southern California.

NOTES

NOTES

NOTES

NOTES